LaRouche Calls Forth the Forgotten Man and Woman Like Roosevelt Before Him

EIR Contents

www.larouchepub.com Volume 45, Number 36, September 7, 2018

LAROUCHE CALLS FORTH THE FORGOTTEN MAN AND WOMAN LIKE ROOSEVELT BEFORE HIM

MANHATTAN PROJECT DIALOGUE

FDR: The Forgotten Man

The History of LaRouche's Call for a Four-Power Agreement To Create a New Bretton Woods

by William Wertz

This is the edited transcript of William Wertz' presentation to the Sept. 1, 2018 LaRouche PAC Manhattan Project Dialogue. The full discussion is available at https://youtu.be/zAR6cluVT-o

I want to tell you a forgotten story, the story of the fight of Franklin Roosevelt against imperialism. Imperialism by the British, imperialism by the Dutch, and imperialism by the French. FDR's vision of the peace after World War II—a peace sabotaged by the British and by their agent, Harry S Truman, who after FDR's death became President of the United States. This is an urgent topic, because the solution to the problems we're facing in the world today requires a New Bretton Woods, which Lyndon La-Rouche has proposed. La-Rouche's proposal is very much in line with the original conception of Bretton Woods as outlined by Franklin Roosevelt and his aide, Harry Dexter White.

Throughout the decades, particularly after Nixon abandoned the Bretton Woods system on August 15, 1971, LaRouche has fought for a New Bretton Woods system. Nixon took the dollar off the gold reserve standard and introduced a floating exchange rate system—as a sharp break with FDR's Bretton Woods system. After that occurred, there was a further devolution in the world economy over the succeeding decades, and in particular in the United States' economy.

President Richard Milhous Nixon, announcing his decision to suspend the convertibility of dollars to gold, Aug. 15, 1971, thereby abandoning the Bretton Woods system.

That fateful decision on the part of Nixon in 1971 led to an increase in free trade policies globally, an increase in globalization in which industry took advantage of "cheap labor" in Third World nations, exploiting that "cheap labor" instead of carrying out a policy of improving the living standards of workers in the advanced sector nations, and developing the skills and living standards of individuals in the developing sector. This was the period in which the idea of a post-industrial society was introduced. Shortly after Nixon made that fateful decision, in comes the Presidency of Jimmy Carter, a project of David Rockefeller's Trilateral Commission. A key aspect of the Trilateral Commission policy was the idea of controlled disintegration of the world's productive economy.

LaRouche has long fought for a restoration of the principles of the Bretton Woods system from his more advanced scientific and economic standpoint. During his Presidential campaign in 1988, he keynoted a conference in January in Andover, Massachusetts, just before the February New Hampshire primary. LaRouche's campaign that year was called the LaRouche Campaign for a New Bretton Woods—that was what he was fighting for. There was a further emphasis upon this concept, in a speech he delivered in Washington, D.C. in 1998, and then an increased emphasis in 2008. From June 2008 through November 2008, LaRouche delivered a number of speeches and wrote many articles on the necessity for a New Bretton Woods.

LaRouche's 1988 Presidential Campaign

In 1988, you still had the Soviet Union and the Warsaw Pact. There were also sovereign nation-states in western Europe. LaRouche proposed in 1988 that the initiating nations for the New Bretton Woods system should be the United States, Japan, and the Western European nations. However, after the collapse of the Soviet Union, things changed.

Europe, for instance, lost its sovereignty with the imposition of the European Union and the Maastricht Treaty. The Soviet Union and the Warsaw Pact no longer existed, and there were further, positive developments with respect to China. By 2008, and perhaps even before that, LaRouche's conception was that there should be a New Bretton Woods system initiated by four powers—the United States, Russia, China, and India. And that these Four Powers had sufficient power to overrule the imperialist policies centered in the City of London. Of course, 2008 was also the year of the financial crisis which hit the world. This was LaRouche's proposal to solve that crisis.

I want to start out with a few quotes from Lyndon LaRouche from the year 2008. On June 12, 2008, LaRouche wrote a paper, "Free Trade vs. National Interest: The Economic Debate about Russia," in which he wrote:

> What must occur soon … must be the formation of an initial organizing committee composed of the governments of the U.S.A., Russia, China, and India, a committee whose agreement to what needs to be adopted as certain common principles of reform, principles which will serve as the needed catalyst for a general, more or less global agreement to a reform committed to certain principles of global cooperation among a majority of the world's nation-states.

On Nov. 11, 2008, he made a presentation titled, "Only My Reforms Can Save the Planet from a Dark Age." There he said:

EIRNS/Philip Ulanowsky

Lyndon LaRouche proposes a New Bretton Woods system in his keynote address, "The New Name for Peace is Development," at a Schiller Institute conference in Andover, New Hampshire, Jan. 30, 1988. Helga Zepp-LaRouche, left, and former Guyana Foreign Minister Fred Wills, right.

So, if we create this seed crystal, of these four nations, and others who join them, we now can have, any time we decide to do it—if the President of the United States says, to the President of Russia and to the President of China, and to the government of India, and some other countries: 'Let's make this agreement!', the United States has Constitutionally, the Constitutional apparatus and the authority, to do this!

Bretton Woods & Physical Science

On November 24, 2008, he wrote "The Truth of Bretton Woods Lies Within Physical Science," in which he said:

> What President Roosevelt had actually proposed was, in all essential features, an anti-British imperialist, anti-monetarist system. His proposed system excluded any defense of that British Empire's predatory interest.

The final piece I want to cite was written earlier, on August 20, 2008, under the title, "New Bretton Woods: Russia's Role in a Recovery." There he wrote:

> Furthermore, while it were desirable that any among Russia, China, India, and other nations would press the United States to initiate the New Bretton Woods reform which I have proposed, it is absolutely indispensable that that reform in in-

ternational institutions actually be initiated as a proffer from the U.S.A....

Roosevelt intended to use that available economic power to eliminate imperialism from the planet's forthcoming, post-war history. Roosevelt's intention, including that expressed by his role in Bretton Woods, was that each nation must have true sovereignty under the needed new reforms, and, at the same time, that all forms of colonialism and its like must be uprooted from the planet....

What President Roosevelt had intended, as I do today ... is a reform of the world's economic and related affairs according to a single, commonly adopted great principle, one conceived in the same spirit as the 1648 Peace of Westphalia.... It must become a new, refreshed body of anti-monetarist, natural, international law of economy, binding together a system of respectively perfectly sovereign nation-states by a common, universal principle adopted in the likeness of a universal physical principle."

painting by Gerard Terborch

Ratification of the Peace of Westphalia (the Treaty of Münster), May 15, 1648, ending thirty years of religious warfare in Europe.

So, that is what Lyndon LaRouche called for back in 2008, and it's what we're calling for today. The United States must play a key role in creating this new system. As he said, it were perhaps indispensable that Russia, China, and India encourage the United States—and in this case, President Trump—to do precisely that.

Standing in the way of this, of course, is the same British Empire which jettisoned Roosevelt's post-World War II vision of peace throughout the world based on a principle of economic development. It wasn't totally abandoned, but the intent was to reverse Roosevelt's policy altogether; particularly his opposition to any form of imperialism, and any form of monetarism. I want to emphasize that Roosevelt's conception of the post-World War II period actually pre-dated the United States' entrance into that war after the bombing of Pearl Harbor on December 7, 1941. Before Pearl Harbor, there was the August 9-12 meeting between Roosevelt and Churchill in Canada—four months before Pearl Harbor. That meeting resulted in the Atlantic Charter., which reflects the principles of the Treaty of Westphalia.

The Atlantic Charter

Here are the key aspects of that Atlantic Charter. There were eight points; we'll focus on five of them:

1. That their countries [The United States and the United Kingdom] seek no aggrandizement, territorial or other;

2. That they desire to see no territorial changes that do not accord with the freely expressed wishes of the peoples concerned;

3. That they respect the right of all peoples to choose the form of government under which they will live; and they wish to see sovereign rights and self-government restored to those who have been forcibly deprived of them;

4. That they will endeavor, with due respect for their existing obligations, to further the enjoyment of all states, great or small, victor or vanquished, of access, on equal terms, to the trade and to the raw materials of the world which are needed for their economic prosperity;

5. That after the final destruction of the Nazi tyranny, they hope to see established a peace which will afford to all nations the means of dwelling in safety within their own boundaries, and which will afford assurance that all the men in all the lands may live out their lives in freedom from fear and want.

This agreement was forced upon Churchill by Roosevelt as a condition for an alliance of the United States and Great Britain to work together to defeat the Nazis. It was a charter that was abandoned very rapidly after the war, thanks to Churchill; as you can see by the kinds of policies confronting us today. There is no policy of regime-change in the Atlantic Charter. There is a commitment to eliminating want throughout the world. Some of these concepts go to the Four Freedoms that Franklin Roosevelt enunciated in his January 1941 State of the Union speech: freedom of expression, freedom of worship, freedom from want, and freedom from fear.

The Bretton Woods system was, in fact, being formulated even before Pearl Harbor. The first proposal for a Bretton Woods system was drafted the Sunday after Pearl Harbor. This first draft was circulated in January 1942. The United Nations was also a conception of Franklin Roosevelt's which effectively went into operation, in the process leading into its post-World War II formation, on December 29, 1941, three weeks after Pearl Harbor. There was a draft called the Declaration by United Nations, referring to the Allies as the United Nations. That document, written December 29, 1941 in the White House, was signed by the initiating parties on January 1-2, 1942.

FDR's Postwar Vision

All of the elements of the post-World War II period were already in motion prior to the United States entering the war. So, what Roosevelt was fighting for, was the peace. He had a conception of the peace which as we will see, was based upon eliminating imperialism. Lyndon LaRouche has made it quite clear that eliminating monetarism and bringing about the economic development of the planet is the basis for cooperation, and for the elimination of imperialism.

Also central, as we will see, to the Bretton Woods conception, was the New Deal. The Bretton Woods system was an effort on the part of Roosevelt to internationalize the New Deal. Another very important factor in this was Roosevelt's Good Neighbor Policy towards Ibero-America. His Bretton Woods idea was that every place in the world, including Indonesia, will be a neighbor. So, it was an internationalizing of the Good Neighbor Policy.

In U.S. history, obviously this goes back to John Quincy Adams and his conception of a community of interest among a family of sovereign nation-states, which was the basis for the Monroe Doctrine. At any rate, those were some of the key factors feeding into the Bretton Woods and the United Nations conception; both of which were already in motion as what the United States was fighting for when it was forced to enter World War II. What was the objective? It wasn't just to defeat the enemy. It was to create a New Paradigm.

I will now go through some important passages from Elliott Roosevelt's book, *As He Saw It*, written in 1946. This book fully confirms what Lyndon LaRouche understood and expressed when he heard about the death of Franklin Roosevelt during World War II, when he was at that point stationed in India. LaRouche often mentions that when the news came that Roosevelt had died, a number of his fellow soldiers wanted to hear what he thought

Lt. Col. Elliott Roosevelt, Algiers, Algeria, December 27, 1942.

about it. So, he arranged to meet with them, and expressed his concern that a great man—Franklin Roosevelt—had just passed away; and a small-minded figure, Truman, was now the President of the United States.

FDR Confronts the British Empire

Elliott Roosevelt documents exactly what his father's interaction with Churchill was during key conferences which Elliott attended at his father's side, starting out when the Atlantic Charter was proclaimed, but then at other conferences that followed.

I had the opportunity in the late 1970s to meet with Elliott Roosevelt on two occasions; I and my now-late wife Marianna. He had moved to Bellevue, Washington in the late 1970s, and we had just moved out there as well. We had two meetings with him. Unfortunately, by that time, for whatever reason, he had lost the sense of fight for what he had expressed in his 1946 book. His book, fortunately, documents a great wealth of what we need to know today, especially in the fight that we must wage today to defeat the British operations that, as then, are directed at the President and at any relationship between the United States and Russia.

So, in writing his book, Elliott Roosevelt begins:

> The decision to write this book was taken more recently and impelled by urgent events. Winston Churchill's speech at Fulton, Missouri, had a hand in this decision, … the growing stockpile of American atom bombs is a compelling factor; all the signs of growing disunity among the leading nations of the world, all the broken promises, all the renascent power politics of greedy and desperate imperialism were my spurs in this undertaking....
>
> And I have seen the promises violated, and the conditions summarily and cynically disregarded, and the structure of peace disavowed.... I am writing this, then, to you who agree with me that … the path he charted has been most grievously—and deliberately—forsaken.

This is already in 1946. Now, what I want to do is review some of the key material in the book with you. This will give you more of a sense of the quality of President we had in Franklin Roosevelt. It's a picture of another America, the America which we must re-establish, and which most people throughout the world, let alone people in the United States, don't know or don't remember, given what's happened over the last 70-plus years.

Roosevelt told Elliott, as reported in Elliott's book,

> Churchill told me that he was not his Majesty's Prime Minister for the purpose of presiding over the dissolution of the British Empire. I think I speak as America's President when I say that America won't help England in this war simply so that she will be able to continue to ride roughshod over colonial peoples.

Churchill's Neck Reddened

Elliott then reports on a discussion between Churchill and his father:

Roosevelt and Churchill confer aboard the USS Augusta off the coast of Newfoundland, Aug. 9, 1941.

Father started: "Of course," he remarked with a sly sort of assurance, "of course, after the war, one of the preconditions of any lasting peace will have to be the greatest possible freedom of trade.... No artificial barriers. As few favored economic agreements as possible. Opportunities for expansion. Markets open for healthy competition."

Churchill shifted in his armchair. "The British empire trade agreements," he began heavily, "are—"

Father broke in. "Yes. Those Empire trade agreements are a case in point. It's because of them that the people of India and Africa, of all the colonial Near East and Far East, are still as backward as they are."

Churchill's neck reddened … "Mr. President, England does not propose for a moment to lose its favored position among the British Dominions. The trade that has made England great shall continue, and under conditions prescribed by England's ministers."

"You see," said Father slowly, "it is along in here somewhere that there is likely to be some disagreement between you, Winston, and me.

"I am firmly of the belief that if we are to arrive at a stable peace it must involve the development of backward countries. Backward peoples. How can this be done? It can't be done, obviously by eighteenth-century methods. Now—"

"Who's talking eighteenth-century methods?"

"Whichever of your ministers recommends a policy which takes wealth in raw materials out of a colonial country, but which returns nothing to the people of that country in consideration. Twentieth-century methods involve bringing industry to these colonies. Twentieth-century methods include increasing the wealth of a people by increasing their standard of living, by educating them, by bringing them sanitation—by making sure that they get a return for the raw wealth of their community."

"You mentioned India," Churchill growled.

"Yes. I can't believe that we can fight a war against fascist slavery, and at the same time not work to free people all over the world from a backward colonial policy."

"What about the Philippines?"

"I'm glad you mentioned them. They get their independence, you know, in 1946. And they've gotten modern sanitation, modern education; their rate of illiteracy has gone steadily down ..."

"There can be no tampering with the Empire's economic agreements."

"They're artificial ..."

"They're the foundation of our greatness."

"The peace," said Father firmly, "cannot include any continued despotism. The structure of the peace demands and will get equality of peoples."

'You Are Trying to Do Away with the British Empire'

In response, Churchill told Roosevelt: "Mr. President, I believe you are trying to do away with the British Empire. Every idea you entertain about the structure of the postwar world demonstrates it."

Later, during the Casablanca conference, I believe, Roosevelt was even clearer in the discussion directly with his son Elliott. He said:

I'm talking about another war, Elliott. I'm talking about what will happen to our world, if after this war we allow millions of people to slide back into the same semi-slavery!

Don't think for a moment, Elliott, that Americans would be dying in the Pacific tonight, if it hadn't been for the shortsighted greed of the French and the British and the Dutch. Shall we allow them to do it all, all over again? Your son

Roosevelt and Churchill confer during the Casablanca Conference, Casablanca, Morocco, January 1943.

will be about the right age, fifteen or twenty years from now.

Then Roosevelt, tired from the day's proceedings, said to his son:

One sentence, Elliott. Then I'm going to kick you out of here. I'm tired. This is the sentence: When we've won the war, I will work with all my might and main to see to it that the United States is not wheedled into the position of accepting any plan that will further France's imperialistic ambitions, or that will aid or abet the British Empire in its imperial ambitions.

He had further discussions with his son. This is another one that I think is very appropriate. He said:

You see, what the British have done, down through the centuries, historically, is the same thing. They've chosen their allies wisely and well. They've always been able to come out on top, with the same reactionary grip on the peoples of the world and the markets of the world, through every war they've ever been in.

This time, we're Britain's ally. And it's right we should be. But ... I've tried to make it clear to Winston—and the others—that while we're their allies ... they must never get the idea that we're in it just to help them hang on to the archaic, medieval Empire ideas.

American foreign policy after the war must be along the lines of bringing about a realization on the part of the British and the French and the Dutch that the way we have run the Philippines is the only way they can run their colonies.

He's just said that the Philippines is scheduled to get its independence in 1946.

Just one further quote from Elliott Roosevelt with respect to his father's comments:

official photo

President Harry S Truman

"The biggest thing," Father commented, "was in making clear to Stalin that the United States and Great Britain were not allied in one common bloc against the Soviet Union. I think we've got rid of that idea, once and for all. I hope so. The one thing that could upset the applecart, after the war, is if the world is divided again. Russia against England and us. That's our big job now, and it'll be our big job tomorrow, too...."

That's precisely the predicament that the British have attempted to put us in today, not in respect to the Soviet Union (the Soviet Union collapsed), but this time in respect to Russia. That's the U.S.-British "special relationship" so-called, in which they manipulate us into conflict with Russia, when in fact, Russian-U.S. collaboration, along with collaboration with China and India, is essential for the world's peace.

Truman Betrays FDR

Elliott Roosevelt describes more of what happened as the war was being concluded, and immediately after the end of the war. He reports that at Yalta, a conference he did not attend, an agreement was arrived at among the U.S., the Soviets, and the UK, of how to handle the defeat of the Nazis. He reports that that agreement was sent by Moscow to Russia's top general, but that neither London nor Washington—that is, neither Churchill nor Truman—sent that agreement to General Eisenhower. Eisenhower didn't know what had been agreed to at Yalta, which created some consternation on the part of the Russians, in particular.

He also reports that there were a number of agreements which Roosevelt had made, based upon his anti-imperialist viewpoint. Roosevelt had a discussion with Queen Wilhelmina of the Netherlands, in which she agreed that the Dutch East Indies (Indonesia) would be granted independence, as was going to occur with the Philippines. As soon as the war was over, British ships brought the Dutch back into the Dutch East Indies. Similarly, in Indochina, British troops brought the French back into Indochina—Vietnam and so forth.

In terms of China, the agreement which Roosevelt had worked out with Chiang Kai-shek was that Chiang and the Kuomintang would join with the Chinese Communists and form a unity government, to be followed by an election. The conditions for that were that the United States would not allow Britain to go back into Hongkong, Shanghai and Canton [Guangzhou], and also that the Soviet Union would agree that it would not take over Manchuria, that Manchuria was part of China.

What happens after Roosevelt's death and after the war is over? British ships go back into Hongkong, Shanghai, and Canton. The entire agreement was invalidated by the combination of Churchill and Truman.

He also mentions that in 1948, there were cocktail parties in Washington, D.C. in which the discussion was about a preemptive nuclear strike against the Soviet Union

France regains control of her Southeast Asia colonies. Shown here, the colonial French Far-East Expeditionary Corps during the First Indochina War (1946-1954).

before it perfected its own nuclear weaponry. This, of course, was the Bertrand Russell policy.

What you see here is a complete betrayal by Churchill of everything Roosevelt stood for, and a reestablishment of imperialism, British imperialism, Dutch imperialism, French imperialism, in the immediate post-World War II period, totally contrary to the Atlantic Charter, totally contrary to everything that Roosevelt intended.

Churchill after FDR's Death

That's very instructive in terms of what we're dealing with today in terms of the British. It's the same British who are carrying out a coup against the President of the United States in order to prevent that President from working with Russia, from working with China. That's the intent. And all of these things, whether it's the Skripal case, whether it's false-flag chemical weapons attacks in Syria, whatever the case, it's all part of the same geopolitical game-plan of the British, of the Anglo-Dutch liberal system.

Now, let's look at the original Bretton Woods conception. As I said, this was already in motion before Pearl Harbor, and it was an attempt to internationalize the New Deal, internationalize the Good Neighbor Policy, and also the Four Freedoms, particularly the Freedom from Want. The first draft was produced in January 1942: In this draft, Harry Dexter White, who worked on this for President Roosevelt, stated that the goal was to "raise the productivity and hence the standard of living of the peoples of the United Nations." He also included what are called the "associated nations," which were those nations, particularly in Ibero-America, which did not declare war on the Axis powers, but which continued to be loyal to the Allies, so they were called "associated nations."

The draft includes the following:

It is true that rich and powerful countries can for long periods safely and easily ignore the interests of poorer or weaker neighbors or competitors, but by doing so they only imperil the future and reduce the potential of their own level of prosperity. The lesson that must be learned is that prosperous neighbors are the best neighbors; that a higher standard of living in one country begets higher standards in others, and that a high level of trade and business is most easily attained when generously and widely shared.

President Franklin Roosevelt (right) promotes his Good Neighbor Policy at a banquet given by Brazilian President Getúlio Vargas (left) in Rio de Janeiro, Brazil, Nov. 27, 1936.

There you have the Good Neighbor policy.

The same 1942 draft also stated that the chief operations of what is now called the World Bank—originally the International Bank for Reconstruction and Development (IBRD)—were to involve the "provision of long-term capital for desirable productive projects" that served "directly or indirectly to permanently raise the standard of living of the borrowing country." According to the January 1942 draft, the Bank could guarantee loans subject to certain conditions: (1) the interest rate of such loans could not be excessive; (2) no more than 80% of the principal and 50% of the interest could be guaranteed; and (3) a loan could not be "for the purpose of repayment of an old loan."

So, you think about what happened with the IMF and the World Bank after 1971: They lent money to repay old loans, so the money didn't really even have to go the borrowing country, they could just wire it over to a bank in New York or the City of London—very simple. The country would never see the money. It wasn't invested in anything productive that could produce new wealth that would allow them to repay any legitimate debt which they had. And of course, the stipulation had been that "interest rates would not be excessive."

FDR's Bretton Woods Intentions

The January 1942 draft also defended tariff protection in poorer countries. Harry Dexter White's March 1942 draft stated that the assumptions that underlie free trade theory were "not valid" and "unreal and unsound."

The draft memorandum prepared for Roosevelt in

May 1942 stressed that one of the purposes of the plan was "to supply the huge volume of capital that will be needed abroad for relief, for reconstruction, and economic development essential for the attainment of world prosperity and higher standards of living." A September 1943 draft emphasized that "large investment sums will be needed to help raise the very low productive level of countries in the Far East, South America, in the Balkans and the Near East." In the same draft, he said rising standards of living worldwide would help generate future "political stability and friendly international collaboration."

That gives you some of the picture. There were other proposals which didn't make it into the final Bretton Woods, which included a debt restructuring mechanism. There were also proposals for capital controls, all of which are measures which certainly Lyndon LaRouche would support in terms of a New Bretton Woods.

The basic point that I would make here, is that we are in a situation where we suffer the consequence of the coup which took place in the United States following the death of Franklin Roosevelt. And LaRouche, over that entire period of time, into today, has been the most committed individual, to ensure that the United States returns to that perspective that Elliott Roosevelt laid out. And I want to go back to what Elliott Roosevelt writes at the end of his book: "I have come to the question: What can we do, we who are not simply officials in the American government but something far more important, which is to say, American citizens? What can we do to ensure our government's return to the path that was charted by Franklin Roosevelt?"

And I would maintain that that's exactly what Lyndon LaRouche has done, as a citizen. He didn't hold any official position. And that's also what we are all called upon to do, as citizens, to return to that perspective, which is a perspective which Americans *can* be proud of, as opposed to many other things which we can't be proud of, particularly as we've come under the influence of the British Empire, and basically serve the purposes of that empire, of the Anglo-Dutch system, against which Roosevelt was completely opposed, and his vision of the post-World War II period was committed to eliminating altogether.

A Second Treaty of Westphalia

I would like to conclude by going through some of the features which are important in terms of what we have to do today. Lyndon LaRouche has emphasized, especially in a peace called "The Coming Eurasian World: Toward a Second Treaty of Westphalia," that there is an elephant in the honeymoon couple's bed. In one citation, he points out that the elephant is defecating on that bed, which does not bode well for the duration of that marriage, or the wellbeing of the marriage.

So: What if, Russia, President Putin, President Xi of China, Prime Minister Modi of India, and President Trump of the United States, all, explicitly, publicly express their commitment to ending all forms of imperialism, to ending the Anglo-Dutch liberal system which has dominated the post-World War II period, until the most recent developments which have initiated by China and Russia, India and other nations, as Diane was citing earlier, the One Belt, One Road initiative of the Chinese; the Eurasian Economic Union initiative of Russia; the BRICS; the Asian Infrastructure Investment Bank; the BRICS' New Development Bank. These are institutions which are not controlled—although they're operating in a universe which is controlled, by this Anglo-Dutch system.

But what if they were all to come forward and say, "this is the common enemy of all humanity," and we essentially commit our nations and we're sure other nations will join us in committing ourselves again to the principle of the Atlantic Charter, or the Treaty of Westphalia, the sovereignty of individual nations, cooperation among individual nations. We are committed to a policy of lifting the living standards of all nations in the world. The Chinese have done that in China, they're committed to doing that in other locations throughout the world. President Trump, very clearly, has an intent to reverse globalization, reverse the damage done by free trade, reverse the policy of post-industrial society, and reindustrialize the United States, creating higher standards of living here. He's not been fully successful in doing that thus far. He's made some progress, which shouldn't be ignored.

But if you've got agreement among the nations, these four powers, you could turn the situation around globally. And the key to that is really going back to the principles of the Bretton Woods system: You've got to have a situation where you have—Lyndon LaRouche has advocated this repeatedly—fixed exchange rates based upon a gold reserve system.

A Credit Policy

And you have to have a commitment to a credit policy, as opposed to a monetarist policy. You have to extend credit for capital exports, to third world nations—what we call "third world" nations, developing nations, undeveloped nations, however you want to express it. That is in the interest of the advanced-sector nation, as well as the developing sector nations, and this is something that Lyndon LaRouche put forward all the way back at the conference in Andover, Massachusetts, in 1988: It's a policy of peaceful, technological transfer to the third world, and he makes the point repeatedly, that if you're doing that, if you gear up our economy, create productive jobs focussing on technology development, for capital goods export, then you're actually benefitting your own economy even before you've been paid for your exports; because you're creating tremendous turnover in your economy, and by expanding it in that kind of way.

And you're creating customers in the third world. If you just impose austerity conditions, as the IMF and World Bank do, then you're basically killing your customer. You're killing your neighbors, most fundamentally, but in addition, you're killing your customers, the people who can be a market for your high-technology exports.

So it's that policy of capital exports, which is absolutely critical. And any agreement among the United States, Russia, China and India, would also involve a commitment—the fundamental commitment is to increase the productive powers in the labor of all nations. That's really even a higher conception that just increasing the standard of living. It's not a question of just increasing consumption. It's a question of increasing the productive powers of the labor force of the total population in all of the respective countries. That goes to Lyndon LaRouche's conception of the need to increase potential relative population-density.

And, of course, it's not just a question of capital exports and infrastructure development, but there should also be an agreement for space exploration, working together to colonize and develop space, and higher forms of energy, including fusion power in particular.

Those would be part of such an agreement. And as Lyndon LaRouche emphasized, what you need to do, is have these four national leaders make a commitment to change the direction of the world, in the direction of the good, as Friedrich Schiller said in his *Letters on the Aesthetical Education of Man*. That's what you've got to do: Change the world by getting it in the direction of the good.

And it must involve the United States: The importance of what I've tried to lay out today, is that many in the world do not have this understanding of the United States. They think that the United States is the imperial power, as opposed to the Anglo-Dutch system and the British. It is true that the United States has been in large part taken over by that system, but that's not the history, it's not the Constitutional intent of the United States. And we have to restore that Constitutional intention, as Roosevelt expressed it. If you do that, then you can have peace through economic development.

Don't Play the British Game

If you don't bring the United States into this combination, if this is not initiated by the United States, then you have precisely the condition which Franklin Roosevelt told his son must be avoided, which is, Britain and us versus Russia. That is the British game plan: You've got to prevent that. And there are many people throughout the world who fall into that trap, including people in Russia, out of desperation. Sanctions are being imposed upon Russia; the same kinds of policies which unjustified, are being imposed on other countries.

That is the British policy, and you have to identify it as the British policy, and you can't give up on the United States. You have to go from the standpoint of a higher strategic flank, grand strategy, which is that you've got to win over the United States. If that doesn't occur, then the world is divided, and that's what will lead to war, as we see in the machinations of the British in respect to Syria and other locations—Ukraine and so forth, throughout the world.

That is what I want to convey: The need for that Four Power alliance as Lyndon LaRouche has emphasized, which *must* include the United States, which means we have to change the United States. And we need allies abroad who are committed to changing the United States back to its original Constitutional intent.

Lyndon LaRouche has been committed to this, certainly upon the very news of the death of Roosevelt in April 1945, and he is a citizen who has fought for this policy. And that's what each of us has to do, as citizens, who have to become informed about the actual history of the United States—one portion of which I've tried to give you today—and commit your life to that fight: That's what Roosevelt did. That's what Lyndon LaRouche has done.

For Further Reading

Forgotten Foundations of Bretton Woods: International Development and the Making of the Postwar Order, by Eric Helleiner, Cornell University Press, 2014.

As He Saw It, by Elliott Roosevelt, Duell, Sloan and Pearce, 1946.

U.S., Mexico Reach 'Fair Trade' Agreement, As the World Moves Toward Principles of LaRouche's New Bretton Woods

by Brian Lantz

Aug. 31—President Donald Trump announced on Aug. 27, that the United States and Mexico had reached a new trade agreement, paving the way for "termination" of the murderous North American Free Trade Agreement (NAFTA). Lyndon LaRouche and this publication have waged a major effort to defeat NAFTA, and in 1991, *Executive Intelligence Review* published an extensive, widely circulated special report, *Auschwitz Below the Border: Free Trade Pact is George 'Hitler' Bush's Mexican Holocaust*, warning that the pact, sold through the Chicago School's "free market" brainwashing, was actually intended to destroy the productive labor force on both sides of the border, benefitting only speculative predatory capital. Lyndon LaRouche's warnings have been fully vindicated in the almost 25 years since NAFTA's passage—on both sides of the border. These disastrous consequences fueled the vote for Trump in 2016. Now NAFTA is over.

In the Oval Office announcement of the new trade agreement, with Mexico's President Enrique Peña Nieto on speaker-phone, President Trump pointedly stated that NAFTA had "bad connotations because the United States was hurt very badly by NAFTA for many years, and it's now a really good deal for both countries." President Trump is clearly aiming at good productive jobs for Americans and Mexicans. Trump tweeted out that same day, "A big deal looking good with Mexico!" The agreement already has the blessings of Mexico's incoming new President, Andrés Manuel López Obrador. As of this writing, Canada and the U.S. continue negotiations for Canada to be included in the new agreement.

The reassertion of national sovereignty and the right to economic development is everywhere in the world today. Helga Zepp-LaRouche, founder of the Schiller Institutes, has issued an international call for the convening of a New Bretton Woods Conference,

led by the four world powers of the U.S., Russia, China and India. Zepp-LaRouche has been the leading international exponent of what has become "The New Silk Road," China's Belt and Road Initiative. She has called on President Trump to join it. In June, Zepp-LaRouche highlighted what she called "the Singapore Model"—the successful talks between President Donald Trump and North Korea's Kim Jong-un—and said that this must be the springboard for similar, new international agreements in global "win-win" cooperation seeking peace and economic development.

Automobile manufacturing in Mexico.

The Agreement: Nation-Building

The new United States-Mexico Trade Agreement can be a positive step along this path, and a major step toward growing international coordination in promoting real economic development across the Americas. To be clear: This agreement is not aimed at China or creating an anti-China "bloc" in the Americas. Witness the British Empire's legacy media grinding their teeth over the successful U.S.-Mexico outcome! Here are details of the U.S.-Mexico agreement as announced to date:

• Forty to forty-five percent of American and Mexican auto and auto-parts workers must earn at least $16 an hour or more to avoid tariffs, breaking the straitjacket of the "cheap labor" NAFTA lunacy that has spread impoverishment on both sides of the border. Mexican auto workers typically make less than $8 an hour, and even less at parts plants, according to the Center for Automotive Research, as cited in *Transport Topics*.

• Under the new pact, there are provisions for new labor rules meant to benefit manufacturing workers. For example, Mexico has agreed to pass a law to provide "worker representation in collective bargaining."

• There are tightened "rules of origin" on vehicles made in the United States and Mexico, so that 75% of their content must be produced in the United States or Mexico, up from 62.5% previously. Seventy percent of the steel, aluminum and glass used to make a vehicle must also originate in North America. For example, American auto companies that assemble their cars in Mexico would also need to use more U.S.-made car parts to avoid tariffs, which would help U.S. manufacturing workers. "Only producers using sufficient and significant U.S. and Mexican parts and material receive preferential tariff benefit." This will aid workers in both countries, shielding them from competition from unscrupulous supply-chain sourcing.

• The nasty "dispute settlement provisions" of NAFTA were weakened. These had featured a system of supranational tribunals staffed by predatory corporate lawyers, which nullified protective national laws.

City of London/Wall Street interests and wage-gouging "businessmen" had wanted to keep these tribunals in place to "reduce the risk of investing." (This would also have been an on-steroids provision of the now deadand-buried Trans-Pacific Partnership or TPP.) Now only oil and gas, energy, and infrastructure companies will retain the right to use dispute settlement panels. However, precisely in this area, incoming President López Obrador has already signaled a suspension of new oil and gas concessions to foreign companies, and will launch an audit of existing concessions for possible corruption.

• Agriculture is the area that is perhaps least changed by the new U.S.-Mexico Trade Agreement. Agriculture remains a disaster in both nations—more on this below.

As a consequence of the agreement, the manufacturing sector is actually strengthened in both the United States and Mexico. Pay scales will rise on both sides of the border, improving the household incomes (the consumer market-basket) of the productive workforce of both countries. Contrary to the fake news from the City of London and Wall Street, this is quite compatible with China's Belt and Road Initiative and the prospect of positive outcomes with U.S. negotiations with China. This is all driving the City of London and Wall Street—and therefore many on Capitol Hill—up the wall.

And in Relation to a New Bretton Woods?

What does this have to do with a New Bretton Woods Agreement?

Cooperation among sovereign nation states is the *sine qua non* of the New Paradigm. A New Bretton Woods Agreement among those nations can only be organized successfully by fulfilling the physical economic requirements specified uniquely by economist and statesman Lyndon LaRouche ("Towards a New Bretton Woods," *EIR*, March 27, 1998). The science of physical economy places the development of the productive powers of labor—the development of the unique creative powers of each and every human individual—at the center. The physically required market-baskets—including consumer, capital goods and overhead market-baskets—must be thoughtfully developed and improved to grow healthy national economies. In his July 18, 2000 paper, "On a Basket of Hard Commodities: Trade Without Currency," LaRouche discusses how productive trade relations among nations must be advanced:

> The key to establishing a reasonably determined standard unit of account for a basket of commodities, is to reject, from the outset, the reductionist input-output presumption of Britain's Piero Sraffa, for example, that consumption might be represented as a process of production of commodities by commodities. We must examine the way in which combined market-baskets of economic infrastructure (such as public works), combined with household consumption and with technologically progressive, hard-commodity forms of increasingly capital-intensive investments in capital goods of production and physical distribution, increases the relative productive powers of labor, as this is to be measured, in physical product, per capita and per square kilometer. *It is that factor of rate of growth, as expressed in hard-commodity terms, which defines the appropriate notion of assignable economic value . . .*

To make possible the rapid increase of such productive powers in every nation, with commensurate upgrading of all national physical economies, exchange rates between national currencies must again be fixed (with minimal fluctuation) by international agreement, as they were under the 1944 Bretton Woods system, thus drying up unproductive currency speculation. Currently irrational, market-driven "global supply chains" and "value-added chains" must be transformed to serve national development priorities. This is not a promotion of autarky; quite the contrary.

Andres Manuel López Obrador, Mexico's incoming president.

Mexico and Labor Power

Consider Mexico. Mexico is the world's ninth largest manufacturing hub and exporting country. Mexico's leading export categories are: $101.7 billion in vehicles (24.8% of total exports); $81.6 billion (19.9%) in electrical machinery and related equipment; $65.9 billion (16.1%) in machinery including computers; $22.6 billion (5.5%) in mineral fuels including oil; and $17.5 billion (4.3%) in optical, technical, and medical apparatus. From a continental perspective, 82.7% of Mexican exports by current market value were delivered to the United States and Canada—fellow members of what had been the North American Free Trade Agreement (NAFTA). Mexico was also the United States' second largest goods export market in 2017, after the European Union.

However, Mexico ranks 57th of 137 nations in hard infrastructure, according to one assessment, and 82nd of 137 nations in education (*World Economic Forum Global Competitiveness Report Index, 2016-2017*). It is clear that Mexico has the manufacturing prowess to build up its own physical economy, specifically to provide for the upgrading of its labor power through an improving production of the market basket for households to maintain and reproduce an ever more productive workforce. Incoming President López Obrador has stated that he intends to "strengthen the domestic market, to try to produce in the country what we consume." He is proposing a doubling of investment in larger infrastructure projects to a total of 4.1% of the national budget, or over $50 billion a year. This is part of a broader program of investment in education, medical, and other infrastructure.

Just hours after his election victory, President-elect López Obrador tweeted about his recent phone call with President Trump: "I proposed that we explore an integral agreement of development projects, which generate jobs in Mexico and with that reduce migration and improve security. There was respectful treatment, and our representatives will speak more." But this is much bigger than the question of migration—as Franklin Roosevelt repeatedly said, a prosperous, developing Mexico means more and better jobs in the United States. There has also been a well-publicized exchange of letters between Trump and López Obrador on cooperation on regional security and economic development of the Americas, which includes the existential task of dismantling the regional drug cartels.

CC/Foxxygrandpa

Meebox all-in-one, desktop computer with touch screen (right) and a Meebox Slate tablet, from the first Mexican company to manufacture a full functioning tablet computer.

Agriculture is another area in which the United States and Mexico have a pressing, shared interest. Mexico's incoming Presidential administration has reasonably stated that it wants Mexico once again to be able to produce its own food—indeed, every country requires this. Consider that until the late 1990s, Mexico was a net exporter of agricultural products, yet today it is a net importer, mostly from the United States. Meanwhile, American farmers have been operating below break-even for decades, and most U.S. farmers are still on their land today only because of their off-*farm jobs.*

As a result of the "market-driven" global cartelization of food supplies, including 25 years of NAFTA, U.S. and Mexican agriculture are so crippled that it will take parity pricing measures and other major efforts to begin to undo the damage. Mexico is now dependent on the United States for corn, a staple of the Mexican diet! Mexican grain farmers had been driven bankrupt under NAFTA, unable to compete with U.S. high-tech agriculture. Now Mexico is also the top market for U.S. corn.

Some numbers: U.S. total exports of agricultural products to Mexico totaled $19 billion in 2017, the third largest agricultural export market for the United States. Leading export categories include: corn ($2.7 billion), soybeans ($1.6 billion), pork and pork products ($1.5 billion), dairy products ($1.3 billion), and beef and beef products ($979 million). Meanwhile, Mexico is now selling to the United States its vegetables and fruit. Mexico exported $25 billion in agricultural products to the United States in 2017, including $6.0 billion of fresh fruit and $5.5 billion worth of fresh vegetables. A number of U.S. agribusiness enterprises now have significant investments in Mexico.

Mexico, the U.S., and China

As in the relationship between the United States and China, if you think in physical-economic terms, you see that the United States and Mexico are joined at the hip. The just-signed U.S.-Mexico Trade Agreement now begins to show that triangular relationship in a new light.

Andrés Manuel López Obrador has invited *both* President Trump and China's President Xi Jinping to his December 1 swearing-in as Mexico's new President. "Speaking with and working with President-elect López Obrador has been absolutely a very, very special time," said President Trump, following the conclusion of the new agreement. Simultaneously, the incoming Mexican President has opened up discussions with China on the possibility of reactivating Chinese railroad proposals which Mexico had previously abandoned under pressure from Barack Obama, and on new Chinese investment proposals regarding Mexican infrastructure. On August 2, López Obrador held a well-publicized meeting with China's Ambassador to Mexico Qiu Xiaoqi, in which the Ambassador expressed China's strong commitment to work with Mexico.

As in other fast-paced developments, including the recent the Trump-Kim Singapore Summit, the Trump-Putin Helsinki summit, and the BRICS summit in Johannesburg, South Africa, the world is undergoing a rapid transformation led by the leaders of nations, acting as sovereign nations outside the established "globalist" institutions. The required reorganization of the global physical economy of mankind can be made to happen in this context.

Meanwhile in China, officials and scholars and are also working to come to cooperative terms with the United States and President Trump. An August 28 article in China's semi-official English language daily, *Global Times*, was titled "Complex Reshaping of Industry Chains Means Sino-U.S. Trade Dispute Likely to Drag On." The article refers to the "revamp of the North American Free Trade Agreement," and argues that there is an intention, on President Trump's part, through such bilateral trade deals, to "foster a high-standard global free trade network to reshape the global manufacturing chain, including between the U.S. and China." Therefore, Hu reasons, "the trade dispute is likely to become a protracted one, because the adjustment of the manufacturing chain is a long process."

Another article, this one an August 20 op-ed in the *South China Morning Post*, argues that President Trump's approach to tariffs is likely part of a "consistent" line of thinking: Trump is using tariffs on China "to indirectly penalize all those American companies which are investing in China as a base for manufacturing with cheap labor and then re-exporting back to the U.S. as well as to other countries." Foreign multinationals, the writer points out, produce 42% of China's exports to the world! While President Trump's tariffs may hurt these U.S. manufacturing companies in China in the short run, the author speculates that over the longer term, Trump is thinking that these tariffs—and the unpredictability of the trade environment generated by the threat of tariffs—will cut U.S. manufacturing investment in China, and—along with other signature Trump domestic measures—will work to bring manufacturing investment back to the United States.

These two articles are another indication that significant currents in China are thinking deeply about President Trump's intentions and America's historic Hamiltonian system of economy, as found in our Constitution. There is thoughtful consideration of the physical-economic parameters that must be addressed to achieve a "win-win" recovery of the scientific, technological, and manufacturing prowess of the United States—which is seen by China as a definite "win-win" goal for achieving world strategic stability and security. China's leadership, led by Xi Jinping, is extraordinarily capable of responding should the United States proffer an agreement to negotiate a New Bretton Woods System.

Towards a New Bretton Woods

The wretched digital Dark Age of the British Empire's monetarist *ultramontane* system, that had supplanted the authority of nation states, is collapsing. Evidence of that has been presented here. Once again, sovereign nation states, inspired by the ideas of the American System of Alexander Hamilton, Lincoln, FDR, Kennedy and LaRouche, and by Xi Jinping's Belt and Road Initiative, are acting on *Westphalian* principles, from the top down. This is at the heart of the "Singapore Model," and this inspired thinking is reflected in the outcome of the U.S.-Mexico Trade Agreement. Nations inspired and cooperating to regain the sovereignty of each, and each with its implicit sovereign power to create its own national banking and credit mechanisms—these are the irreplaceable means by which each can mobilize its own nation's unique productive, creative powers to contribute to the advancement of mankind.

President Trump and the other "Big Four" national leaders of China, India and Russia, can be caused to act for a New Bretton Woods Agreement, and Trump will be enabled to act domestically for LaRouche's "Four Laws," if the American people now crush the British Empire's Mueller/Russiagate coup attempt before the November midterm U.S. elections. A "consistent" policy perspective on President Trump's part, will include Lyndon LaRouche's Four Laws, starting with the return to Glass-Steagall and a national credit institution to provide trillions of dollars in credit to restart the U.S. economy from within. Mexico is willing, China is waiting; the whole world is watching.

In his official "Letter from the President to the Speaker of the House of Representatives and the President of the Senate," dated Friday, August 31, President Trump states, "… I intend to enter into a trade agreement with Mexico—and with Canada if it is willing, in a timely manner, to meet the high standards for free, fair, and reciprocal trade contained therein.…" The U.S. Congress now has 90 days to consider and vote on the U.S.-Mexico Trade Agreement before President Donald Trump signs it into law.

Our Task: Stop an Impeachment Congress

by Susan Kokinda

The following is an edited transcript of the opening remarks by Susan Kokinda to the LaRouche PAC weekly Fireside Chat on August 20, 2018. The full discussion is available at https://youtu.be/15550XLBpKQ

I want to address the question of the midterm elections from the standpoint slightly longer than an election cycle—well, actually, a lot longer—2,500 years. I want to go back to the great poetic drama written by Aeschylus, *Prometheus Bound*, which was written in about 500 B.C. Some of you are familiar with the basic outline: The god Prometheus aligned himself with the human race against the Olympian leader god, Zeus. Zeus wanted to wipe out the whole human race: He decided 2,500 years ago that there were too many of us. You can see that the idea of overpopulation has a long, long history.

Prometheus defended mankind by giving mankind the gift of fire, and Zeus punished him by chaining him to a mountainside for all of eternity, with an eagle picking out his liver.

I think it's important to read this beautiful poetic drama. Prometheus gave mankind much more than just the gift of fire. It's really a metaphor for man's ability to comprehend universal principles, because what Prometheus says is: I gave him knowledge of the seasons, so that man could develop agriculture; I gave him knowledge of letters, so he could pass on learning; I gave him technology, so he could build buildings; and husbandry to harness animals, so we wouldn't live like animals or be beasts of burden. That's the human outlook.

What Zeus represents is the imperial outlook, the principle of the oligarchy—the idea that the few have the right to determine life and death over a domesticated herd which is denied access to advances in technology, denied access to the essential quality of being human. I really do encourage people, if you haven't read this, it's easy to get on the Internet, you can get a Dover Edition for a couple of bucks.

Our Task: Stop an Impeachment Congress

It gives you the insight you need to see what the real battle between paradigms is—right now—in the midterm election. The midterm elections are not a fight between parties; they are a fight between paradigms. It would be nice if you could go into the voting

Painting by Giovanni Francesco Guercino (Barbieri).
Above, "Prometheus Animating with Fire the Clay Figure of a Recumbent Man."
Right, Prometheus and his brother Atlas, both punished by Zeus.

EIRNS/Bryan Barajas

EIRNS/Robert Baker

Candidates Kesha Rogers (left), Independent for U.S. Congress (TX-9); and Ron Wieczorek (right), Independent for U.S. Congress (SD) are campaigning for a new Bretton Woods international monetary system.

you can't. Except for the campaigns of Kesha Rogers in Texas and Ron Wieczorek campaign in South Dakota, where you have candidates explicitly supporting the new paradigm. Instead it's going to necessitate that we address the population from the standpoint of this larger principled fight.

Go back to Zeus and his punishment of Prometheus: any political figure or movement, which challenges the control of the oligarchy has the wrath of Zeus brought down upon them. Obviously, that's what's happening to Donald Trump. He's there to challenge the policies of the modern-day Olympian gods, the British Empire. He's against their policies of globalization, and perpetual war, and free trade. Even worse, Donald Trump laughs at them! That makes them very angry.

This is the same thing that happened to our movement in the 1980s, when Lyndon LaRouche was working with Ronald Reagan to overthrow the oligarchy's doctrine of Mutual and Assured Destruction (MAD) with Reagan's adoption of the Strategic Defense Initiative and attempts to actually implement it. But even worse, LaRouche wanted to bring the gift of fire to a mass political movement, that is, to arm the population with the scientific knowledge of physical economics, and the

EIRNS/Stuart Lewis

Federal task force conducts raid on LaRouche's Campaigner Publications offices in Leesburg, Virginia, Oct. 6, 1986.

power to willfully shape the policies of the nation toward a better future.

Not only were these ideas a threat in the abstract, but we had a movement, a citizen-candidates' movement of thousands and thousands of candidates, some running for local election, some running for U.S. Senate, Congress, governor, and a few were beginning to win primary elections. Well, at that point, Zeus assigned one of his imps, named Robert Mueller, to bring the wrath of the Olympian gods down on our movement, with the same kind of witch hunt that we're seeing today being carried out against Donald Trump.

As threatening as our movement was in the 1980s, as threatening as Trump's victory was, and is, the real threat to Zeus today, is what LaRouche called for a decade ago: that is, a four powers agreement among the United States, China, Russia and India, to bring down the British-run monetarist system and replace it with a New Bretton Woods, based on the principles of LaRouche's economics.

We can now see that the new configuration of powers on this planet—those four nations and their current leadership—threatens to end the control of this British oligarchy once and forever.

Russia, China and India are increasingly in sync around the New Silk Road Spirit, as Helga Zepp-LaRouche has described it. We have Trump's relationship with Xi Jinping, reaffirmed today in a tweeted Presidential statement, in which President Trump confidently projected that we will be able to work out the trade disagreements with his "good friend, the great Xi Jinping." So those parts of the Four Power agreement are in place. When Trump succeeded in going to Helsinki, meeting with President Vladimir Putin, well, that was the last piece of the puzzle moving into place.

The gods on Mount Olympus are not happy. We know the hysteria of the escalation they've carried out since Trump's trip to Helsinki—the intensification of the coup process which Barbara Boyd went through very thorough in last Saturday's Manhattan Town Hall dialogue.

The latest intensification of the effort to break up any Four Power agreement, to break the United States primarily from moving into this new configuration, is the threat of a false-flag chemical attack in Idlib, Syria. In her weekly Schiller Institute webcast, "Brits Preparing a New False Flag in Syria, Citizens Must Choose: War or New Silk Road," Helga Zepp-LaRouche went through that very thoroughly.

So, we have to escalate, and the elements of that escalation are the continued and intensified circulation of the Schiller Institute petition for a New Bretton Woods conference, brought about by those Four Powers. There will be a conference in New York City on Sept. 13 on this very subject. We have to bring this battle into focus, in the fight for the midterm election, and we have to make absolutely clear that this is the fight between two paradigms.

Several weeks ago, LaRouche PAC issued a national leaflet and this should be the ammunition that we use throughout the country, with one voice, as we intervene into these midterm elections. It's on our website, entitled "Countdown to the 2018 Mid-Term Elections: We Must Take Charge Now!" I'm just going to read the opening, in case people haven't seen it:

> On November 6, 2018, Americans will go to the polls. This will be the most consequential election of our lifetimes. If the current crop of crazy "Resist" Democrats take the House, and the present equally crazy free trade, new Cold War

loving faction of Republicans join them, President Trump will be impeached and the policies of George W. Bush, Barack Obama, and Hillary Clinton, and worse, will re-emerge, triumphant. The world will be back on a course for war with Russia and China—a war which the human race will not survive.

Those are the consequences.

We are challenging people to take charge, to assume the role that our Constitution envisions. We have to set the agenda for this election. We're calling on citizens and candidates alike to pledge themselves to three critical big game-changers:

1. To not support the impeachment of President Trump. Shut down the coup attempt and prosecute those who are trying to carry it out.

2. Adopt the full body of LaRouche's Four Laws.

3. Work with Russia and China and other nations on areas of mutual interests—in particular, counterterrorism, joint ventures for infrastructure, and exploring space.

Those points have to be the defining litmus test in this election.

Lessons Learned in Michigan Organizing

Let me give you a little background in terms of the origins of this particular leaflet, because we, here, in Michigan and the Midwest, were somewhat frustrated in terms of our ability to affect the primary process, which here in Michigan concluded on Aug. 7. We do have a Trump movement, and some decent people won nominations for Congressional seats and Senate seats. But now, of course, they face the challenge of getting elected, and anybody who's sane here in Michigan knows that that's not going to happen on party lines. The Trump people know this. In Michigan's Aug. 7 primary, 140,000 more Democrats turned out than Republicans.

There's a key race here in Michigan in the 11th Congressional District—this is two women, here in the Year of Woman. One of them, Lena Epstein, was one of the architects of Trump's victory in Michigan; the other, Haley Stevens, was the chairman of Barack Obama's auto task force. There you have it: a clear Trump-versus-old-paradigm standoff in this election. But again, more Democrats turned out than Republicans in the primaries.

President Trump speaks to hundreds of autoworkers at the American Center for Mobility in Ypsilanti, Michigan, March 15, 2017.

The 11th Congressional District is unique in another respect. This is the district where Bill Roberts, our LaRouche PAC-backed candidate ran for Congress in 2012 and 2014, as a Democrat. In 2012, in the Democratic primary, campaigning very prominently to impeach Barack Obama, he got 40% of the vote in the Democratic primary. Not quite what Kesha Rogers was able to do, by winning her primary in Texas, but still a reflection of a similar revolt among the constituency in this Congressional District. That is part of the audience that we have to address.

What we discussed with LaRouche PAC's Treasurer Barbara Boyd, as we came out of the primaries, is that while there were some decent candidates, the level of discussion in the primaries was abysmally low. Even the decent candidates didn't bring up the really fundamental issues that are going to move people, especially the blue-collar voters. Barbara said, just intervene as if we were running for office ourselves, and that's where the idea for this leaflet came from. We have to take charge, and we have to set the agenda.

What we have planned here in Michigan is kind of a land and air assault with this midterm leaflet. Last Saturday, we went up to Lansing, the state capital. The Republican Party was having its convention to finish off their slate and pull together for the elections and so on. We just stood outside the convention hall, got out hundreds and hundreds of leaflets, and signed up tons of

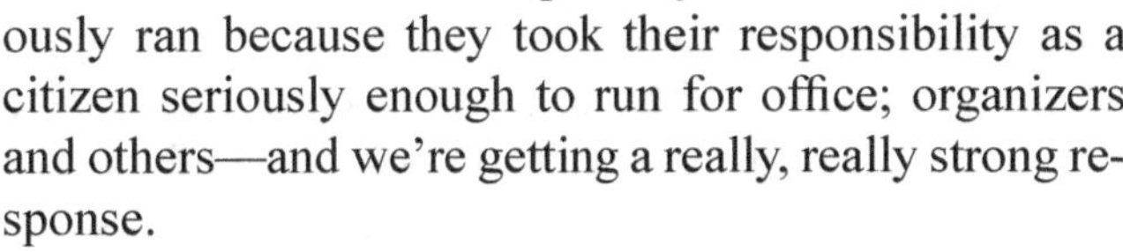

Lena Epstein, Republican nominee campaigning for U.S. Congress from Michigan's 11th CD.

contacts, with an extremely high recognition that this race is not about "Republicans versus Democrats." In fact, some of these Republican delegates were saying they didn't trust the Republican Party—for good reason—there are some pretty lousy people running on some of the state ticket here in Michigan.

Set the Agenda!

But that's not our focus. Our focus is to ensure that we set the agenda in this election. We got out scads of leaflets. We're calling on new supporters that we're meeting in the field, as well as our veteran activists, to take this leaflet, saturate the political landscape with it. People can go door to door, they can get it out on social media, they can go to political events and leaflet with it. Already we're starting to get some of the political layers that we met at the convention and elsewhere pledging to circulate our LaRouche PAC statement. We're using Facebook very aggressively to reach out into these political layers. Former candidates, people who lost their primary elections but obviously ran because they took their responsibility as a citizen seriously enough to run for office; organizers and others—and we're getting a really, really strong response.

People are responding, sending back emails, phone numbers for follow-up. We've already had one candidate for office, and one former candidate for state legislature calling back for more intensive discussion of LaRouche's policies and how we're approaching this. Many people are thanking us profusely for this outlook and asking for more discussion in order to grapple with what they admit are "big ideas."

We're also seeing it in the field organizing. The response that we're getting from people, is a recognition that what's important in terms of swinging these midterm elections in the right direction, is really about people *don't know*. In other words, they know that if it's party politics as usual, they're going to lose. It's what they *don't* know, that they're eager to find out. This means the policies that our movement has put forward.

I think one of the things that people should be attuned to, is that President Trump is going to be out on the campaign trail,—I don't remember the number of days—between now and the midterm elections. The states that we know he's going to are Nevada, North Dakota, South Dakota, Tennessee, Missouri, Montana, and Kentucky. If you live in one of those states, make sure that you are getting the White House email notifications of where these events will be. With 24 to 48 hours' notice, you can print up leaflets and go to these rallies. There will be tens of thousands of people at these rallies—saturating these layers with these marching orders, *and* getting as many contacts as possible, is one really concentrated area of intervention that we can focus on.

Get in touch with us, if you want help in coordinating this kind of activity.

We are getting close to just a two-month countdown into the midterm elections, and the key, really, is to break the controlled environment. We cannot let the media, or the two major political parties set the agenda.

Fascism with a Democratic Face

Breaking the controlled environment is a crucial element in terms of how we have to address those layers of the population who have been subjugated to the brainwashing of the enemy's outlook. Anybody who's stepped outside their house in the past two years and tried to talk to a "Never Trumper," knows that there's a phenomenon of hysteria and insanity within these layers, which I don't think we've seen in living memory.

The production line of B24E Liberator heavy bombers at Ford's huge Willow Run plant in Ypsilanti, Michigan, January 1, 1943.

What you're actually seeing is what the British and their psychological warriors called "Fascism with a Democratic Face." It is something this organization wrote about extensively over decades—what the British were faced with: how to take a population, particularly in the United States, which had mobilized to win World War II and defeat fascism, which had provided— especially here in the Midwest, the "Arsenal of Democracy" which revived our economy in the greatest economic recovery up to that point, such that we could actually defeat Britain's Nazi threat, how do you take that population and over however many decades it's going to take, how do you get a significant section of them to willingly adopt policies that will reduce their standard of living, kill their future, destroy their nation, and possibly lead to thermonuclear war?

And that will be the final result, if we get an impeachment Congress in 2018.

LaRouche addressed this phenomenon of Fascism with a Democratic Face, extensively, in a lengthy pamphlet in 1974. While some of the tactical aspects of some of his writings are no longer relevant today, the universal scientific principles he addresses are more relevant than ever before.

Key to brainwashing a population, is the creation of a controlled environment in which the victims are brought—willingly or otherwise—to reject any concept of universal principle. This gets back to Zeus versus Prometheus. To brainwash people, you embed people in an artificial world—today called a "narrative"—where one's entire worldview is controlled by the idea and the power imposed by the oligarchy. Once

you live in that world, then you're allowed to make "democratic decisions," constrained to that world.

The anti-Trump movement today is really the personification of Fascism with a Democratic Face. Yes, there are decent Democrats, but if they're going to subject themselves to the impeachment, warmongering, and anti-growth insanity of the party leadership, they're going to be just as culpable as those who are consciously pushing these policies.

I want to take a moment and introduce you to some of the ideas that LaRouche was putting forward in the 1970s, to better understand this phenomenon, of how to break a population in such a way to create this kind of movement. He starts with a quote which seems pretty obvious on the face of it. "The basic difference between mental health and mental disease is the distinction between reality and fantasy." Well, that does seem obvious, but, really, the question is: What is reality? I think most of you on this call know it's not CNN. But it's also not Fox TV or Alex Jones. In other words, not-CNN— the negative of CNN—is not reality.

Reality has to be defined from a Promethean standpoint, that is, how man knows the universe and acts on the universe. Nothing which operates below the principled fight between an oligarchical system and a truly human system is reality! We addressed this question in a very fundamental way in the recent class series that Dennis Speed and Will Wertz just presented.

They made the point that reality can be found only in the relationship of human beings to the physical universe. LaRouche's economics is the study of how human beings relate to the universe and discover the noösphere,

in the way LaRouche discovered it, so they can improve it. I would say that that class series is really basic training for people who are going to be intervening into the midterm elections. It's available on https://discover.larouchepac.com/ and people should put themselves through this— it's like boot camp, an eight-week training process. You're going to have to condense the time-frame because that's about what we have until the midterm elections, now.

Back to LaRouche's discussion of how to shape the thinking of the population: It's not surprising how LaRouche locates the segment of society which is most susceptible to sanity. He says,

It might be imagined that the sanest person is one who works with his hands, since he is obliged to prove constantly that the mental processes guiding his hands are in an appropriate correspondence to whatever laws of nature determine the actual results obtained.... Sanity, the appropriate perception of real connections in the world, involves the thinker's assuming personal responsibility for the consequences of his concepts in respect *to those persons who act upon them in connection with lawfully determined processes.*

This is where the blue-collar vote for Trump comes from. Blue-collar workers, farmers. These are people who have a connection to reality. You can't go into some fantasy world and think that you can plant corn in January in Montana, and that somehow, you're going to have a crop. There's enough of a connection to the real world, such that you maintain a layer of the population which was able to respond as it did in the 2016 election, and give Trump the margin of victory, which gave him the Presidency.

Then the question is, who are the people who are less susceptible to sanity, less connected to reality? The further you get away from productive employment, or living in a productive household, the more controllable you are. Look at the composition of our economy today—I think the manufacturing base of our society is somewhere in the 20% range—you have a huge pool of people, who are floating around in a state of mind in which reality never knocks on their door.

LaRouche takes it one more step, and this is what I want to really stress in terms of how people think, in terms of intervening into this midterm process. He gets into the nitty-gritty of the actual brainwashing, and what LaRouche says, is:

> The small group operates exactly like a brainwashing group, particularly if established within a controlled aversive environment. Its smallness precludes its attempting to exert any meaningful influence on the major issues of material consumption, leisure, political institutions and so forth. Consequently, it is compelled to limit its deliberations to secondary issues, to alternatives as defined in the limits for demands established by the aversive authority controlling the larger environment.

An entire layer of the population has been decoupled from reality. It's not just fake news. It is removing people from any relationship to the real universe of causal action. The fact that the causes of the crisis facing the nation cannot be addressed in this kind of process, is the fundamental aspect. The population has descended into smaller and smaller identities and issues, which will never, ever fundamentally change anything.

The minute you step back from the big issues, as we define them in this midterm election leaflet, you cede territory, due to the enemy's aversive environment. And if you go back to the 1970s, when LaRouche was writing these, what were the big issues? The big issues were the 1971 destruction of the Bretton Woods system. The British began to seize control of the *entire world financial system.* Unless that is addressed, you are never going to be able to address the economic problems in your country. In the 1970s, you also had the assault on our productive culture, with the rise of the zero-growth movement, anti-population, and deindustrialization. This is now firmly embedded in the entire culture, and unless you take that on, you've ruled out the most fundamental principle which defines reality, which is man knowing and improving upon nature.

This is what's wrong with the Democratic Party and the trade unions as institutions today. They stopped taking on those big battles, pretty much after the assassination of John F. Kennedy, Martin Luther King, and Bobby Kennedy. They might fight for a piece of a shrinking pie, but they've accepted the aversive environment. Frankly, there's no Republican Party; there's a Trump movement, and then there's neo-con allies of the Democratic Party on the other side.

Take Charge, Break the Controlled Environment

This defines what we have to do in the midterms. We have to have a conscious understanding that we're breaking the controlled environment, the aversive environment of the British Imperial system. You can't fight with people inside that environment. You've already discovered that if you've tried to talk to a hysterical anti-Trumper, on the issues that are "allowed" by the media. We have to break people from the brainwashed axioms of the British Empire. That's the aim of this national leaflet.

You have to identify for people the face of the enemy: It's the British. It's not the "deep state" or the "new world order," or "socialism," or "big government." People need to understand that the Democratic Party of Franklin Roosevelt and John Kennedy was destroyed by the British and transformed into the party of Fascism with a Democratic Face. But it's the British game.

You have to fight from the Promethean standard of reality; that is, fight for the Four Powers and the New Bretton Woods. Fight for the principles which we outline in this campaign leaflet and take charge. That is the only way that we are going to ensure that an impeachment Congress is not elected. Fight like Lyndon LaRouche always has done, from the standpoint of universal principles, as embodied in all of our current campaigns.

EIRNS/Lissie Maria Brobjerg

LaRouche PAC organizing.

Xi Jinping, Aesthetical Education, and Africa— And the Deep Moral Crisis of the West

by Helga Zepp-LaRouche, Chair of the German political party 'Civil Rights Movement Solidarity' (*BüSo*).

Sept. 1—While the political establishment in Europe still sees itself as the sole possessor of the only true wisdom regarding the alleged superiority of "Western values," more and more so-called "ordinary citizens" have long realized that there is an ever wider gap between the official depiction of events by politicians and the media, and reality as it presents itself in different aspects of life. The negative media coverage of China and the New Silk Road might also be *fake news*. In fact, between these so-called "Western values" and the concept of the "New Silk Road," there is a clash of two diametrically opposed sets of values and two completely different images of mankind.

For the past ten years, and more intensively over the past five, China has been involved in many infrastructure projects as part of its Silk Road Initiative, including railway lines, industrial parks, hydropower plants, and the industrialization of agriculture in Africa. African heads of state, as well as the populations, have a completely new sense of self-assurance: for the first time they see a realistic chance of overcoming poverty and underdevelopment in the foreseeable future. Thanks to Chinese aid, a number of African states now aim to achieve a very good standard of living for their entire populations in the medium term.

On the eve of the FOCAC summit, which 53 African leaders are expected to attend in Beijing, Ghana's ambassador to China Edward Boateng, in a *Global Times* commentary, expressed the spirit of the New Silk Road which has taken hold of the African continent: "The Chinese believe it is possible for a country like Ghana to be transformed into a technologically devel-

Global Times

Edward Boateng, Ghana's ambassador to China.

oped and modernized economy within a generation;"

In the year since he was accredited ambassador in China, Boateng has visited more than 16 provinces and many cities to study the success of the "Chinese economic miracle." As he summed it up in the *GT* commentary, "I believe that Ghana could use China as a mirror to reflect on how we can achieve a similarly successful development path. I note, in particular, the fact that China has been transformed into a major economic and technology powerhouse, and how it has still been able to maintain distinct aspects of its rich culture."

Boateng emphasized that building a strong manufacturing base, investing in human capital, widespread discipline, a serious approach to problem-solving at all levels, unceasing innovation, economic growth, and infrastructure development have all contributed to the success. He further stated that China's "discipline of purpose" and confidence in its cultural/traditional and humanistic values is part of a mindset which would greatly benefit Ghana. He recalled that Ghana was the first African country to throw off the yoke of colonialism, and that its founding president, Dr. Kwame Nkrumah, had been the father of Pan-Africanism, which sits deeply in the conscience of Africa and the Africans.

Colonial Thinking in the West

Of course, Europeans would have been able to develop the African continent infrastructurally and industrially, just as China has done for ten years now. What prevented them was the persistence of colonial thinking, as expressed in the IMF's brutal credit conditionalities and the World Bank's anti-development policies. While China and the African countries emphasize their deep-knit friendship, the few Europeans who are beginning to wake up to the gigantic changes in Africa seem to worry, at best, that China and other Asian countries are securing access to Africa's raw materials.

During his recent trip to Africa, which took him to seven countries, German Development Minister Müller criticized the EU's and the German government's

China upholds its classical tradition, but Germany does not, writes Zepp-LaRouche. Here, Chinese youth in Beijing.

Africa policy, which has consisted of erecting walls against the refugees. "In the next ten years, more will be built in Africa than in the whole of Europe in the last hundred years," stressed Müller. He said he had seen in Mozambique the great resources that this continent has at its disposal; the Chinese, Indians, Japanese, and Americans are already here, he said—only the Germans are not, and they are missing out on many opportunities.

Chancellor Merkel, who was traveling at the same time to Senegal, Nigeria and Ghana, where she met up with Müller, had the sudden realization, after meeting Ghana's President Nana Akufo-Addo, that the EU would only have a prosperous future if it were possible to "manage" the question of migration and the question of a partnership with Africa; otherwise she does not believe that the cohesion of the EU can be guaranteed.

But it remains to be seen what this "managing" means concretely, and whether it goes beyond the cynical policy of the past, which was only arrangements with African governments on stopping migration and on the construction of refugee camps, which Pope Francis has already compared with concentration camps. The latest proposal from the German government's Special Representative for African Affairs, Günter Nooke, which seriously proposes a new colonialism (*Reuters*, Aug. 29), does not bode well: "Why not set up special development zones there, in which countries give up their sovereign rights for 50 years, and the EU could perhaps guarantee the legal framework for in-

Stop Club of Rome Genocide in Africa!

by Lyndon H. LaRouche, Jr.

with a new preface by Helga Zepp-LaRouche

is now available in flowing text ebook and paperback editions from Amazon.com and Google Play Books.

Today, the ideas presented in this book are rapidly being adopted and implemented around the world by more and more governments and institutions. Most importantly, the concepts in this book actually work! Poverty *can* be eliminated from the list of problems facing mankind.

This and dozens of other important EIR books are now available from Amazon.com and Google Play Books.

vestments by foreign companies?"

Even more outrageous, however, is the article "Towards 'Eurafrica'" in the *Bayernkurier* of Aug. 26, which essentially repeats the horrendous theses of Stephen Smith's recent book *La Ruée vers L'Europe (The Rush to Europe: Young Africa on the Way to the Old Continent)*. Africa is experiencing the "most rapid population growth" the world has ever seen, the article states; there is a "population explosion" and a "youth surplus." With their development aid, "the rich countries are shooting themselves in the foot," Smith writes in his book. "By helping poor countries reach the threshold of wealth which allows people to start leaving in the first place, they are subsidizing migration." He views the "return of protectorates" (which Nooke also calls for), as the only way to ward off the "storm surge of migrants," and believes the EU could make deals with African "dictators" [to stop migratory flows in exchange for becoming protectorates].

Obviously, the *Bayernkurier* is not above mobilizing in the spirit of Björn Höcke (of the Alternative for Germany party), barely seven weeks before the state legislative election in Bavaria. In other words: development aid, let alone investment, should be avoided—it is better that people stay poor and die as soon as possible. Are these the "Christian values" with which the *Bayernkurier* wants to support the election campaign of the Christian Social Union Party?

A totally different message was delivered by China's leading news agency, *Xinhua* on August 31. It reported as the top news of the day that President Xi Jinping, in a letter to professors of the Chinese Academy of Fine Arts, stressed the importance of aesthetical education for the sound physical and mental development of youth. Aesthetical education, he wrote, plays an important role in the formation of a beautiful mind, a beautiful soul.

And even though one would never suspect this in the illusory world that the mainstream media in Germany is trying to maintain, the world is moving swiftly in the direction that Lyndon LaRouche and his association have fought for, for decades. China today is implementing the policy that we had published in a book on the industrialization of Africa in 1980, and have since

As a work of classical art, the Winged Victory of Samothrace *(2nd Century B.C., ancient Greece, now in the Louvre in Paris), symbolizes the aesthetical education essential for the formation of a beautiful mind—almost lost in Europe today.*

presented in many conferences, and in the state election campaign of the BüSo in 2009 under the slogan: Hesse's future lies in Africa!

And the emphasis on aesthetical education by President Xi also proves this author's thesis, presented in a speech in New York in April 2017, that there is a great affinity between the image of man and the aesthetical education method of Confucius, and those of Friedrich Schiller.[1] The difference is that China upholds its classical tradition, while in Germany we have moved far away from our classical-humanistic culture. But perhaps it is not too late—we just need to bring Nicholas of Cusa, Kepler, Leibniz, Bach, Beethoven, Schiller, and von Humboldt, to name a few, back to life in the minds and the souls of our youth. We must place more emphasis on their aesthetical education, rather than on preparing them for a career to earn as much money as possible, and to satisfy all desires in the here and now. If you, dear reader, can agree with these lines, you should become active with the Schiller Institute.

zepp-larouche@eir.de

---

1. https://larouchepub.com/eiw/public/2017/eirv44n16-20170421/08-19_4416.pdf

Brits Preparing New Chemical Weapons False-Flag Attack! You Must Choose Now: War, or New Silk Road

This is the edited transcript of the Schiller Institute's August 30, 2018 New Paradigm webcast with the founder of the Schiller Institutes, Helga Zepp-LaRouche. She is interviewed by Harley Schlanger. A video of the webcast is available.

Harley Schlanger: Hello, I'm Harley Schlanger with the Schiller Institute. Welcome to our weekly webcast, the discussion with Helga Zepp-LaRouche, the founder of the Schiller Institutes.

We're seeing a real intensification of the battle between two paradigms: the old geopolitical paradigm which refuses to die and go away; and the emergence of the New Paradigm centered around the Chinese initiative around the Belt and Road, but also with our insistence that this can be the basis for the establishment of a New Bretton Woods system. Clearly, this is something the British are out to destroy, to stop. The latest is the word from the Russian General Staff and the Syrian government that they've picked up a plan by the British to launch a new, false-flag chemical weapons attack in Idlib province, Syria, and blame it on Assad and launch another strike.

Helga, this is a replay of an old

www.whitehelmets.org/en

UN/Loey Felipe

Karen Pierce, Britain's Representative to the UN, lies about Assad preparing a chemical weapon attack, while covering for another such attack by the British-directed White Helmets.

www.whitehelmets.org/en

policy, but it looks as though, based on Tuesday's discussion at the UN Security Council, this is what the British intend to do.

Helga Zepp-LaRouche: Yes. About five days ago, the Russian Foreign Ministry and the Syrian government said that they have evidence that the White Helmets were involved in bringing poison agents to two regions around Idlib, and that as the Syrian army is progressing to take over Idlib, which is the remaining nest of terrorists, this new provocation is being prepared, with the White Helmets having the usual role of being ready to then film the victims suffering from the attack which they carried out themselves.

Tuesday, in the context of the UN Security Council meeting on Syria, the British ambassador to the United Nations, Karen Pierce, made an unbelievable speech. Anybody who wants to see how the British function live, in their own name, can and should watch the speech by the British UN ambassador. In her speech, Pierce baldly asserted that Russia's warning is just another instance of Russian propaganda and is a smokescreen—that Assad is preparing once again to bomb his own population in Idlib.

This has no credibility. There is such a thing as truth. The role of the British in the previous two strikes against Syria, which was based on White Helmets fake news, has been exposed. Who the White Helmets are, has been the subject of many, many articles around the world. This British ambassador, in front of representatives from most of the world, and most of the world's media outlets, is repeating these lies. This is so outrageous.

Stop British False-Flag Attack in Syria

The Schiller Institute has released a statement, "The World Must Unite to Stop the British False-Flag Chemical Attack in Syria," characterizing the nature of this operation. Please help us to circulate it as widely as possible. It is very important that this be circulated right now: That is the only way this operation can be stopped. This has to be an international mobilization, in which people all over the world point to the role of the British being behind it, in a new attempt to create an incident in Syria. The British intent is not only is trying to sabotage the hope for a peaceful settlement in Syria, but also to drive another wedge between the United States and Russia—between Trump and Putin.

This *unbelievable* ambassador who, after this performance, really does not deserve that title, also said that there should be no reconstruction in Syria, no Marshall Plan, no Brussels Plan, and no return of refugees. It's hard to imagine anything more war-hawkish and blatant. We are witnessing a British intelligence operation, and an attempt, at the UN, to try to sell it to the world.

I appeal to all of you: Help us circulate this statement, which was endorsed by the national campaign of Kesha Rogers. Although she is running as an Independent candidate in Texas for Congress (9th C.D.), her campaign has national importance, because she is opposing Al Green, who is the Democrat Party leader of the impeachment drive against Trump. It's very important that you take note of Kesha's action on this. Circulating this statement may be the only way to stop a horrible repeat of U.S., U.K. and French attack on Syria, which could be an attack creating much loss of life and creating misery for many, many others. Help in this mobilization. This kind of provocation could easily go out of control and lead to a larger war, if not a nuclear war. This is very, very serious.

Schlanger: And the British couldn't be more blatant than that is in fact what they intend. We've seen this twice before—actually, three times before—there were false-flag operations in Syria. Helga, you pointed earlier to an incredible speech made by General Sir Nicholas Carter, Chief of the General Staff of the British Army, who said that Britain has to be prepared, the West has to be prepared for war with Russia: This is the British game plan.

Zepp-LaRouche: Yes. This was a speech which he made in January. It is a bloodthirsty speech giving a whole list of the supposed intentions of Russia and British counter-intentions, stating that the West had better get ready because, in his words, "We may not have a choice about conflict with Russia."

This is obviously what these people are risking, because they realize their system is about to blow. The old paradigm of geopolitics is losing—it's losing big. The only thing these people have left is to have these kinds of provocations and try to sabotage, and ruin, and cause havoc, but they have absolutely no constructive idea to offer, and that is why they are losing.

The British Couldn't Be More Blatant

Schlanger: These provocations run parallel to the operations to impeach Donald Trump. A new set of exposures came out this week in Congressional hearings. Bruce Ohr, who previously had been the number four person in the Justice Department—a department deeply riddled with corruption from the old Bush and Obama networks. Ohr was forced to reveal that he was not only a back-channel for the British "former" intelligence operative Christopher Steele, but that he knew that Steele's report was false, when the FBI used it to go before the FISA [Foreign Intelligence Surveillance Act] Court.

It seems, Helga, that this should be just another nail in the coffin in the Russiagate operation.

Zepp-LaRouche: I think that that is very clearly one of the reasons why this British Empire faction, which is not just the City of London, but also the intelligence chiefs of the Obama Administration (what people sometimes mistakenly call the Deep State is really part of this trans-Atlantic, British Empire apparatus) is on an escalating war path right now. They are exposed.

This could turn immediately into criminal prosecution. Trump is quite feisty, with his tweet today saying there were crimes committed. He tweeted, "Ohr told the FBI it [the Fake Dossier] wasn't true, it was a lie and the FBI was determined to use it anyway to damage Trump and to perpetrate a fraud on the court to spy on the Trump campaign. This is a fraud on the court. The Chief Justice of the U.S. Supreme Court is in charge of the FISA court. He should direct the Presiding Judge, Rosemary Collier, to hold a hearing, haul all of these people from the DOJ & FBI in there, & if she finds there were crimes committed, and there were, there should be a criminal referral by her."

I think that's going to happen. The true story is that the aim is to sabotage the relationship between the United States and Russia, which Trump is trying to repair. He did a pretty good job in Helsinki in starting that process.

I think this has a very good chance of prevailing. The momentum is clearly not in the direction of the people who are behind the conspiracy of Russiagate, and Russiagate has long turned into a "Muellergate." Trump is hanging in there. Despite all problems caused by the pressure he is under, problems that we should not ignore, this guy is hanging in there, against this apparatus: This is quite something. I really urge people to go to our websites: look at the recent material written by Barbara Boyd, a leading expert on this whole question. She has provided all the ammunition you need, the material you need to know, so please help circulate her reports. This is what people don't know, especially in Europe. In Europe, most people have no inkling as to the nature of this operation. So please get these reports, study them and circulate them.

Forum on China-Africa Cooperation

Schlanger: The media continue to denounce Trump's demand for an investigation of the FISA Court warrant. President Trump keeps pointing to the fact that the FBI knowingly lied, using a dossier prepared by someone who was paid for by the Clinton campaign. Furthermore, Bruce Ohr's wife Nellie, was working for Fusion GPS, which hired British intelligence's Christopher Steele to do the dossier! Bruce Ohr is the Justice Department official who was brought in for testimony a few days ago. You couldn't have a more compelling case of collusion between the British and the Obama intelligence operation.

What you said about Trump is quite clear: We've never seen a President so openly taking on this estab-

The closed-door testimony of Justice Department official Bruce Ohr before House investigators Tuesday revealed new details about the FBI information-gathering steps both prior to and

lishment. That's why we're seeing this war-provocation escalation in Syria now, the attempt to get a new false-flag operation going.

Helga, one of the other aspects of the conjuncture, is that parallel to all these escalations, the Forum on China-Africa Cooperation (FOCAC) conference in Beijing China will be starting on September 3. This is extremely important in terms of shaping the potential for the Belt and Road Initiative.

Zepp-LaRouche: Oh, yes. I think I'm very safe in predicting that this China-Africa summit will establish a completely new standard of international relations. In this, the fifth anniversary of the announcement of the Belt and Road Initiative, numerous articles have been published in the Chinese media pointing to the very, very impressive success of this New Silk Road, which now involves signed treaties and deals with about 80 countries. In the last five years, a trillion dollars in trade was exchanged among the participants, with much more to come.

There is a continuity of the Belt and Road Initiative with the UN Agenda for Sustainable Development

Zimbabwean President Emmerson Mnangagwa (left, with scarf), arrives in Beijing to attend the FOCAC Summit.

FOCAC bird theme sculpture.

Chinese President Xi Jinping (right) greets Ethiopia's Prime Minister Abiy Ahmed Ali.

Chinese President Xi Jinping holds talks with South African President Cyril Ramaphosa at the Great Hall of the People, Sept. 2, 2018.

Egyptian President Abdel-Fattah al-Sisi (left, front) arrives in Beijing for a state visit and to attend the FOCAC Summit.

2030—which has the aim of eliminating all poverty on the planet (to which China has given great momentum and leadership) and with the African Union's Agenda 2063—announced in 2013 as its next 50-year plan. I advise everyone to read that plan, it's not generally known. It is a very, very ambitious plan that demonstrates the intention of the African nations to become completely modern, fully industrialized, and able to provide good living standards for all the people of Africa, based on high technology and the frontiers of science. It's quite wonderful and is absolutely coherent with the Belt and Road Initiative.

Now, just prior to the start of the FOCAC summit, a great number of African leaders are already in Beijing, or on their way, with large delegations. The Presidents of Zimbabwe, Ethiopia, Senegal, Nigeria, and many other nations will be attending.

What struck me the most, is that when these leaders describe the relationship between the continent of Africa and China, they always say, not only is it one of mutual benefit and win-win cooperation, but most of them emphasize, as the Chinese do, that the relationship is one of friendship, of a deepening friendship. This is really wonderful. I remember that British Prime Minister Winston Churchill once said that there is no such thing as friendship among nations—countries only have "interests" that they pursue. This is a bestial kind of view. The new Chinese-African friendship and common future reflects the true nature of mankind: that people are capable of loving other cultures and nations, when there is a commitment to discover the beauty of each other's cultures.

Nigerian President Muhammadu Buhari with German Chancellor Angela Merkel in Nigeria, Aug. 31, 2018.

Eritrean President Isaias Afwerki (right) with German Minister of Economic Cooperation and Development Gerd Müller, Aug. 24, 2018.

It really is a mirror for us in the West to see what we have done wrong. Europe could have done what the Chinese are doing now. Africa is Europe's neighboring continent. The poverty in Africa, the refugee crisis—all of that could have been prevented, if European nations had been committed to investment in African nations, as China is now doing.

Bonds of Friendship

It is quite interesting, that now, in light of the clear signs that China and Africa are creating new bonds of friendship, that the Europeans are now waking up. Italy is a different case: the new government has begun fruitful cooperation with China with respect to Africa. But what about Germany? Chancellor Angela Merkel is now on a three-country tour in Africa. She went to Senegal and will go to Nigeria and Ghana. The only thing

reported so far is that she is trying to make agreements to somehow prevent people from emigrating to Europe and that she's not having any success.

The three countries—Senegal, Nigeria, and Ghana—are among those nations with many people wanting to leave. I don't have exact figures, but depending on which country you are taking about, youth unemployment ranges from 40 to 60 percent and consequently, half to two-thirds of the population wants to emigrate—to the United States, to France, to other European countries, or to other African countries. Unless this high youth unemployment is remedied, many young people do not see any way to remain in their own nations. That's why Merkel is not having any success.

Germany's Development Minister, Gerd Müller, is approaching this somewhat differently. He just visited seven countries and will be meeting up with Merkel in Ghana tomorrow. After those visits, he said that he was greatly impressed with the rich potential of Africa, with its resources. He attacked the EU and even the German government for not understanding the potential Africa represents. He reported that China, Japan, India, and America are already investing in Africa, and Germany is not. He made a big appeal for that should change.

The wind *is* changing. There was a program on the German Deutschlandfunk (DLF), a radio network, relatively close to the government, interviewing someone who said, "No, German industry must have direct investment in Africa." The wind is shifting, but the West is just not getting it, yet.

The Wind is Changing

The European and American establishments are so full of themselves, so much on their high horses, that they think they are the beautiful and wonderful people, that they know it all. In Europe, it is expressed in a Eurocentric point of view. These Europeans are completely oblivious to the changes that have already taken place. In a certain sense it's a tragedy: Europe has so much to contribute, such as the Italian Renaissance and German Classical culture—all these absolute treasures. But we see nothing of use coming from the present financial and power elites.

Therefore, we must really mobilize. The Schiller Institute is truly necessary: The only way to prevent a clash between the two paradigms—which would lead to a new war, and possibly the extinction of civilization—is to get the Western countries to join the New Paradigm, and rather than fighting it, and to bring in the best of our western traditions. However, those best traditions need to be re-activated and actualized, Only the Schiller Institute is proposing that a just new world economic order, a new governance in the world combined with a new cultural Renaissance that will bring forth the best traditions of all cultures. Join the Schiller Institute, become a member of this Renaissance movement. It is urgently needed!

Schlanger: I would suggest that people order copies of the special reports published by *Executive Intelligence Review* and the Schiller Institute: *The New Silk Road Becomes the World Land-Bridge*, *Extending the New Silk Road to West Asia and Africa*, and *The New Silk Road Becomes the World Land-Bridge, Vol. II*. These three reports will give you a much deeper understanding. We're not just talking about building railroads, we're really talking about elevating mankind to an entirely new self-conception.

Helga, you mentioned the situation in Europe. There's a lot going on: Merkel and others are going to have to wake up. There is the immigration crisis, elections are coming up in Bavaria, the German government's popularity is continuing to fall; there were riots in Chemnitz over the last couple of days. All this is really pushing the political class to come up with something, isn't it?

Zepp-LaRouche: Yes. But look at their ideas. Look at the new proposals by German Foreign Minister Heiko Maas, who is saying that Europe must become more independent from the United States. Now, I'm not against that, were it based on the idea of sovereignty and redefining what should have been redefined at the point of the German reunification in 1990. That opportunity was lost. The promises made to Gorbachev, to not move NATO to the Russian border, were broken. There are many important reasons to review these mistakes. However what Maas is proposing really won't work; it's a Eurocentric idea. He wants to build a European army, which is not going to go anywhere.

Czech President Milos Zeman just proposed dropping the sanctions against Russia, because the sanctions are hurting both sides. Zeman said it's not only the Czech Republic, it's Slovakia, Austria, and Italy also

Czech President Milos Zeman

PRAGUE, August 30. /TASS/. During a meeting with ambassadors and other diplomats in the Prague Castle on Wednesday evening, Czech President Milos Zeman called for the removal of anti-Russian sanctions, the CTK news agency has reported.

opposing these sanctions. This proposal by Maas only increases the centrifugal forces in Europe. Many countries want to have better relations with Russia and with China.

The Stakes Are Very High

There is a proposal by French President Emmanuel Macron to reset the relationship with Russia. We need to look at that more closely. Mr. Macron sometimes makes very eloquent and interesting speeches, but we will have to see what he does. I will give him the benefit of doubt, but I don't want to uncritically praise something which hasn't really materialized yet. There is a great deal of confusion on these issues. What is lacking is really a vision for the future.

This lack of vision and future oriented policy is already creating disasters. Look at what happened in Chemnitz, it is really terrible: A 35-year-old man was killed. The announced suspects were a Syrian and an Iraqi. That led to many angry demonstrations. There were neo-Nazis and hooligans. But there were also a lot of ordinary people—not all the demonstrators were Nazis, absolutely not! There were a lot of regular people. Even the *NZZ* [*Neue Zürcher Zeitung*], the major Swiss daily, said this reflects a much deeper

EIR/Eli Santiago

LaRouche PAC organizers mobilizing to stop the witch hunt against President Trump, and for a New Paradigm for humanity.

crisis, and that is true. The dissatisfaction of the masses of the population with the policies of the neo-liberal establishment is quite profound.

The national elites have completely lost touch with the interests of their own people. Such angry demonstrations are sure to come. In this case, the police were completely incapable of keeping control. My biggest worry is: What will happen were an uncontrolled financial collapse to occur? There already is capital flight out of the emerging markets—a collapse of the currencies of Argentina and Turkey, the corporate debt bubble—all these things are looming over us.

Therefore, our mobilization to put a New Bretton Woods on the agenda, with the United States, Russia, China and India (and possibly Japan) taking the lead, is the only way to solve this at the necessary higher level. Other countries will join us, and the nations of the world will go back to fixed exchange rates, to a credit system and bury for good the casino-gambling type of economics. This is very urgent. We have a petition , which I urge you to sign and circulate. We need to establish a higher level of reason. The combination of these four countries is absolutely crucial (possibly adding in Japan as a fifth) to having enough power to counter and overcome the power of the City of London and Wall Street.

It's Not a Timeless Situation

Join us in mobilizing with this petition. My nightmare is, what will happen if the world does not go to a New Bretton Woods system in the short term, and an uncontrolled repeat of 2008 ensues, but on a much larger scale. Then, the Chemnitz rioting would just be a very tiny foretaste of what could happen, because once people can't get food, medicine—the things they need to survive—chaos could erupt very quickly.

So, we're not in a timeless situation. We're really in a very urgent countdown. In the United States, it's obvious that the midterm elections could really turn the tide for the entire world in a negative direction if people who are for the impeachment of Trump and defend this conspiracy are elected to Congress. Most are Democrats, but many are Republicans, so I'm not calling for any one party to be voted for. American voters will really have to look at each individual candidate. If a candidate is defending this Russiagate coup, that candidate should not be in office.

We are in a very urgent time of mobilization. Don't sit on the fence, get active. People all over the world can get active with the Schiller Institute.

Schlanger: Just to put an exclamation point on that, the proposal that your husband drafted initially for the Four Power Agreement, leading towards a New Bretton Woods, has been discussed and studied by governments all over the world, by think tanks, and others. There's no fundamental objection to it, except from the neo-liberals and neo-conservatives who want war and the chaos that comes with it, rather than see an emergence of a New Paradigm.

Again, I think it's incumbent on people to go to our website, study these ideas and see exactly how far-sighted Lyndon LaRouche and Helga Zepp-LaRouche have been in defining this new potential.

And Helga, I just want to bring up one final point, which I think goes to the difference between a collaboration and a confrontation: We've been hearing a lot about North Korea, the continuation of the Singapore model, the attempt to use that to resolve differences, and the attack on it coming from both parties, as you mentioned, from the media, the attempt to belittle Trump in this. But he exercised another example of leadership yesterday, when he made the statement that the United States will not be resuming joint military exercises with South Korea,— again, going right at the fragility of the situation that includes the British push for a false-flag attack in Syria: I just wonder if you have any final comments on the overall significance of what we have to do now, that it's really up to the people to be mobilized around these ideas.

Food for Thought

Zepp-LaRouche: The media have been talking for some while that the whole Singapore summit is falling apart, that the denuclearization of North Korea isn't working. Obviously, there are some problems, as Trump asked Secretary of State Mike Pompeo to postpone his trip to Pyongyang. But when Defense Secretary James Mattis announced that the United States and South Korea were resuming their joint maneuvers, Trump, the next day said, "no," there is no reason to spend large sums of money on joint U.S.-South Korea war games. The Blue House [the Presidential mansion] in South Korea said that they were not informed by the United States that these maneuvers should take place, and they're looking forward to the upcoming North Korea-South Korea summit in Pyongyang. The Koreans have no interest in seeing the peace process being sabotaged, and that includes, emphatically, the South Koreans.

People should not fall for the media spin on the Koreas.

I would like to end on another note: There was an interesting article quite recently in *Global Times*, saying that the next generation of the West will determine the future.

The author presents an interesting analysis which, however, could be deepened. It is interesting, however, to see this in a Chinese publication. The author says the first generation in the postwar period was absolutely committed to the common good, to the idea that there must be a balance between individual freedom and the common good of society. That generation was focussed on reconstruction and a commitment to ensuring that the terrible horrors of the 20th Century, the Nazi period, would never be repeated. Then came a second generation of people who grew up with more wealth, they had "everything." The tendency toward neo-liberalism became stronger. Now we have a third generation. The key problem with that third generation in the West after the Second World War, is that they have absolutely no idea of the future.

I think that that is the key problem. If you don't have a vision, an idea why you should organize your life in a moral fashion, that you have to develop all your potentialities to be capable of service to humanity, if that is missing, you have hedonism, you have drug addiction, you have autism as a result of excessive videogaming, Internet, social media, all of this. You have basically a youth who are totally crippled!

And it is my view—that either you find enough people in the West to help the Schiller Institute and join with us to remedy that, or it is just a question of time, before the West will lose out, simply because we didn't take care of our own youth. So join with the Schiller Institute to help us to remedy this. I want to give you that as food for thought—something to think seriously about.

Schlanger: And I'd like to urge our viewers to join us next week, when we'll be getting a report from Helga on the extremely important summit of the Forum on China-Africa Cooperation.

Helga, thank you, and we'll see you next week.

Zepp-LaRouche: Yes, till next week, I hope.

Why Accusations Against China for 'Debtbook Diplomacy' Are a Hoax

by Hussein Askary and Jason Ross

Askary and Ross are the authors of the 260-page Special Report, Extending the New Silk Road to West Asia and Africa, *published by the International Schiller Institute in November 2017.*

Aug. 22—Panic is spreading in certain circles in the trans-Atlantic region, dominated by the City of London and Wall Street, over two factors: (1) that their bankrupt monetary and financial system, including the Euro system, is clearly in the final phase of its disintegration process; and (2) that an alternative, new paradigm in international economic and political relations has spread over large swathes of the planet thanks to China's Belt and Road Initiative (BRI); the BRICS nations' new development policies; the Shanghai Cooperation Organization's expansion; the alliance between the China-spearheaded BRI and the Russia-led Eurasian Economic Union; and the China-Africa economic cooperation process.

Rather than doing the obvious, encouraging the United States and Europe to join the new paradigm, these forces are going to dangerous lengths to block the way for the new paradigm and prevent the United States itself from joining it. Their attempts are based on disinformation and lies.

Their anti-China slanders and fabrications all originate in the hysteria emanating from London and Wall Street over the successful efforts of President Donald Trump to build friendly and cooperative relations with both Russia and China, efforts which threaten the geopolitical designs of the British Empire and its financial elites.

The corrupt mainstream mass media, hired academic institutions, and think tanks are at work to invent new lies, sometimes packaged as academic studies, and coin new terminology that is then used by powerful political institutions in a futile attempt to stop the new paradigm. Russia is, of course, a permanent target of defamation and economic sanctions, but China is gradually beginning to receive the same treatment. The latest such lie being peddled through academic and quasi-academic institutions is that of China's "sinister plan" behind the BRI to set "debt traps" for poor and developing nations. "Debt trap" and "debtbook diplomacy" are the new catch-phrases that are now frequently used to portray China's policies.

The term "debtbook diplomacy"—with the meaning that China builds influence over other nations by deliberately causing them to take on more debt than they can handle—was coined in a May 2018 report, commissioned by—and custom designed for—the U.S. State Department and written by Sam Parker of the Harvard Kennedy School's Belfer Center for Science and International Affairs.[1] This report was then used by the U.S. State Depart-

---

1. "Debtbook Diplomacy—China's Strategic Leveraging of its Newfound Economic Influence and the Consequences for U.S. Foreign Policy," Sam Parker, Harvard, May 2018. Before his Harvard assignment, Parker, according to his biography published in the report itself, served as the Special Assistant to the Assistant Secretary for Public Affairs at the Department of Homeland Security. And, "As an academic fellow at U.S. Pacific Command, he wrote a report on anticipating and countering Chinese efforts to displace U.S. influence in South Asia and Oceania." The report is based on old British geopolitical concepts and prejudices against China. All articles referring to the term "debtbook diplomacy" have been published since mid-May 2018.

Cargo ships at the Hambantota Port in Sri Lanka, built by China Harbour Engineering Company and Sinohydro Corporation. It opened in 2010.

ment to ring alarm bells all over the world about the potential impact of China's Belt and Road Initiative. The report's author, Sam Parker, is not known to have any expertise in economics or to have written anything about the economies of China or other developing countries.

From the outset, Parker clearly exposes his Mackinder-inspired British geopolitical worldview,[2] writing: "Debtbook diplomacy is by itself neither an economic tool nor a strategic end. Rather, it is an increasingly valuable technique deployed by China to leverage accumulated debt to advance its existing strategic goals. Three strategic targets for China's debtbook diplomacy would be: filling out a 'String of Pearls' to project power across vital South Asian trading routes; undermining U.S.-led regional opposition to Beijing's contested South China Sea claims; and supporting the PLAN's [People's Liberation Army Navy] efforts to break out of the First Island Chain into the blue-water Pacific."

The most outrageous irony here is that Parker is (falsely) accusing China of the very crimes that the City of London, the International Monetary Fund and trans-Atlantic banks have been blatantly committing for decades—the use of usurious debt to impoverish developing nations and to coerce them into military and geopolitical concessions.

Hambantota: the Deceitful and Only Example

China's relationship to the Sri Lankan port of Hambantota is always held up as a "template," as Parker suggests, of how China intends to treat other nations. But, Hambantota is the only example that the critics of China can come up with. The three stages of the development of the project, including the building of a container terminal, cost a total of $1.1 billion. It was not a Chinese idea, however, but a Sri Lankan government plan to ease the pressure at the only major port of the country, the Colombo Harbor Port, and to build an international port and industrial zone at a safe distance from the civil war raging in the north. This plan dates to 2002, long before the BRI was conceived. Building power plants and industrial zones to foster economic

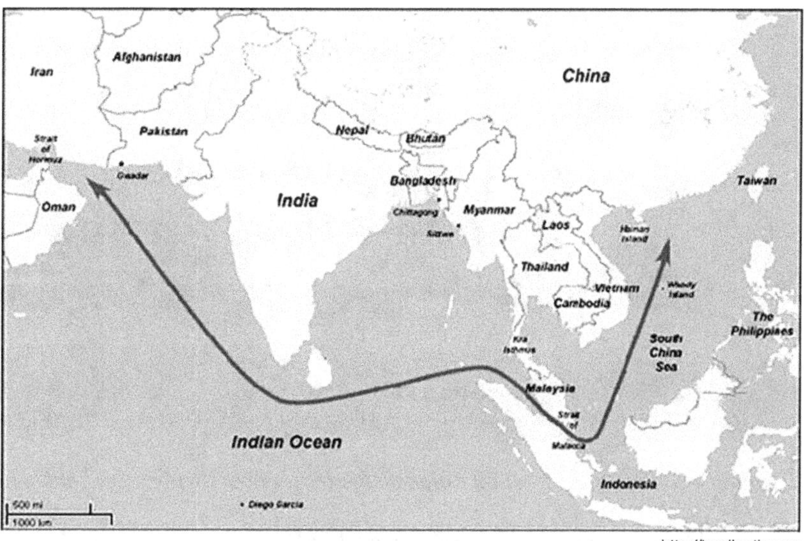

http://tamilnation.co

When the Hambantota Port story is taken out of its context, it sounds like China built a port in a desolate, empty beach on the shores of nowhere. In fact, Hambantota is located just 6-9 nautical miles from one of the busiest and most important commercial shipping lanes on the planet.

activity was part of the "Regaining Sri Lanka" economic program.

The critics take the Hambantota Port out of its national and global context—another glaring case of "lying by omission." They assume, first, that Sri Lanka will always continue to be a poor country with no industries, no agriculture, and no other modern economic activities that would necessitate the existence of modern infrastructure, such as this port.

Second, most of the commercial shipping lines between East Asia and Europe pass a mere six to nine nautical miles south of the southern coast of Sri Lanka—a fact rarely mentioned, which makes clear the potential benefit from this huge volume of global trade passing through these waters, but currently without affecting the economy of Sri Lanka. This port holds a great potential for future development of shipping services, trans-shipment, and building of industrial zones benefitting from the available transport means to world markets.

Construction of the harbor began in 2008 by the China Harbour Engineering Company and Sinohydro Corporation. Eighty-five percent of the project was financed by a loan provided by the China Export-Import Bank. The port was formally opened for commercial use in 2010, but usage was below expectations. In 2016, faced with poor revenues and significant financing costs from the port's construction, the Sri Lanka Ports Authority (SLPA) signed an agreement whereby China Merchants Port Holdings Company (CMPorts), a Chinese state-run enterprise, took a 99-year lease of 70% of the

---

2. Sir Halford John Mackinder (1861-1947), one of the founding fathers of modern British imperial geopolitics.

cc/Adbar

Terminal building at the Mattala Rajapaksa International Airport, Sri Lanka, located near the Hambantota Port.

port, and 85% ownership of the port and industrial area, with the obligation to continue investing in upgrading the facilities there. The Chinese company would invest $700-800 million more in developing the port area. The purpose of the agreement was to relieve Sri Lanka from the burden of the debt.[3] Was Sri Lanka deliberately given loans for a project doomed to commercial failure, with the intent of then seizing the port as payments came due? Parker would have you think so.

But is this the only reasonable conclusion? To the extent this specific example exposes a general trend, it exposes the indifference of international financial institutions and their allies to the aspiration of developing countries to eliminate poverty and economic backwardness. Parker himself reports that after a devastating, decades-long civil war, "Sri Lanka reached out to Japan, India, the IMF, the World Bank, and the Asia Development Bank to fund the construction of a major port in the undeveloped backwater of Hambantota, but was denied funding amidst concerns about human rights and commercial viability." China did not turn down Sri Lanka, and in fact helped that nation achieve a goal it had already sought.

One important aspect of economics that modern day economists and journalists don't understand, is that the value of infrastructure is not primarily its ability to provide a monetary return; rather, it is infrastructure's role as a key factor in the development process of any modern economy, helping raise the productivity of the economy of the entire nation. The "return on investment" lies not in fees forced upon users of the infrastructure utilities, but from the revenues of productive industry and agriculture that uses these utilities.

Were the low port utilization simple miscalculations on the part of the Chinese, poor investments that did not work out as planned? If China has paid billions of dollars for a failed airport and a failed port project, which it now owns, should we expect China's adversaries to be laughing their heads off at that nation's clumsiness, rather than being alarmed and panicked by such failures? But it is the future that will show whether these investments were failures, not security analysts such as Parker.

Treating Developing Nations as Minors

It is quite remarkable to see—when European and American politicians, researchers and writers talk about developing nations—that they subconsciously speak on behalf of those nations as if the people of those nations were children incapable of speaking for themselves. This is a very revealing aspect of the still deeply ingrained colonial mentality, or the "white man's burden" prevalent among trans-Atlantic oligarchs.

W. Gyude Moore, Liberia's former Minister of Public Works and a Deputy Chief of Staff to that country's president, recently interviewed on a podcast, spoke to the African view of Chinese financing from his vantage point as the official who negotiated many infrastructure projects with the Chinese side, offering his response to the way China is frequently portrayed:

> When China is presented as if it is this big, bad actor, who is acting in bad faith and loading countries with debt, it almost takes away the

---

3. The agreement, however, does not stipulate that the debt of $1.4 billion to the China Ex-Im Bank would automatically be cancelled, rather the CMPort would deposit $973.658 million (85% of the total $1.12 billion) in the bank account of the SLPA. Whether the Sri Lankan government uses this sum to repay the original debt to China is up to the Sri Lankan government. Details of the agreement can be found here: http://www.cmport.com.hk/EN/news/Detail.aspx?id=10007328

W. Gyude Moore, Liberia's former Minister of Public Works and a Deputy Chief of Staff to President George Weah.

agency of the countries. It's almost as if African countries are naive or they don't understand what is happening to them and China is basically pulling wool over their eyes. This almost infantilizes Africans and African leaders … Because of the limited amount of money that's coming from international financial institutions, countries like Liberia have to look elsewhere.... One of the few countries that is actually available to talk to countries like Liberia that may not have the best credit record, having just had almost $5 billion of their debt waived, is China.... For a country like Liberia, you couldn't possibly depend only on the World Bank or the African Development Bank to be able to finance your infrastructure—that would not have happened.[4]

Expanding on the relationship between debt distress and investments in the future, he added: "To be able to repay their debt, their economies have to be in a place where they're actually generating revenue, and without infrastructure [this is not possible]. It's almost like the chicken and the egg."

Moore responded to the use of the example of the Sri Lankan port of Hambantota:

Everybody brings up the port in Sri Lanka, but

China has given out billions of dollars in debt. And in my view, that the port in Sri Lanka is the only example that people can give, shows that this Sri Lanka example, this one instance, cannot be seen as the be-all and end-all of how China engages its partners.

The Real Debt Trap

Historically, the British Empire was, and still is, the debt-trap master. Its methods have been copied in the post-1971, post-Bretton Woods era by such British-controlled institutions as the International Monetary Fund and World Bank, to shackle nations with unpayable debt, in order to loot them, destroy their physical economic productive capabilities, and finally force them to give up their national sovereignty. Under the 19th-century, British-dominated imperialist world order, as in the case of the post Bretton Woods system, money is treated as a "global" commodity controlled by private interests, rather than a political tool controlled by sovereign governments, the issuance of which is intended to promote the productivity of society and the general welfare of its citizens.

One pedagogical example from the 19th Century is the way the British and their French allies shackled Egypt with massive debt, forcing it gradually to abandon its natural and labor resources to be taken over by the British, losing its sovereignty over economic and financial policies, and finally being occupied by Britain militarily.

In the early 1860s Egypt was a relatively large producer of cotton to the world markets. With the start of the U.S. Civil War in1861, the production of cotton in the Southern States drastically shrank and the price of cotton in the international markets skyrocketed. Egypt was suddenly awash with revenue from cotton sales and started borrowing from British and French banks to further develop this cash-generating crop. In 1865, when the Civil War ended and American production of cotton resumed, prices collapsed. Egypt suddenly found itself in a financial crisis. The British and French banks, however, continued to loan money to Egypt at ever higher interest rates to service and increase the debt.

In the meantime, the Suez Canal was being built (1859-1869), and controlled by the French Suez Canal Company, which had received a concession offered by Khedive Said Pasha. According to the 99-year lease agreement, the French side financed and built the canal in return for the majority of the shares in the company. The Khedive was offered 44% of the shares.

When Said Pasha's successor, Khedive Ismail Pasha,

<hr>

4. The China-Africa Podcast, Aug. 4, 2018, "An Insider's View of the China-Africa 'Debt-Trap' Debate."

Isma'il Pasha, Khedive (Viceroy) of Egypt and Sudan from 1863-1879.

Dredging equipment in use in the construction of the Suez Canal, January 1, 1859. The canal was completed in 1869.

Evelyn Baring, c. 1895.

was unable to pay the debt to the British banks in 1865, he handed over all the shares in the Suez Canal Company to them as a payment for part of the debt. But the problem did not stop there. In previous years, the Khedive had expropriated large swathes of agricultural land, especially in the Nile delta, from Egyptian farmers, forcing the latter to work as serfs in his new cotton and sugar plantations to produce more cash crops to pay the debt. When he defaulted again in 1876, he was forced to hand over the plantations to the British banks. The British and French bankers actually moved into the Egyptian government's offices (in IMF-style today) to run the financial and economic policies directly. One such British banking "adviser," officially called the "Controller-General in Egypt," was Evelyn Baring of the famous British family of that name. As best described by Rosa Luxemburg,[5] "European capital has largely swallowed up the Egyptian peasant economy," where the lands, the serfs, the government and the Khedive became the property of empire.

When a group of Egyptian military officers staged a military revolt in 1882, Britain used it as an excuse to occupy the country. In 1883, Baring (the Earl of Cromer from 1901), went from being the debt collector to becoming Consul General of Egypt, the de facto ruler of the country, with his term extending until 1907. Britain's occupation and control over the economy of Egypt continued, practically, until 1952, when republican forces led by General Gamal Abdel-Nasser overthrew the backward Khedive system, but did not nationalize the Suez Canal Company (then entirely controlled by the British) until June 1956.

There are abundant, similar examples in the post-Bretton Woods era (since the early 1970s) in which the financial interests of the trans-Atlantic system used the political and military clout of the United States, Britain and Europe to set similar traps for developing nations. The cases of Brazil and Mexico in the 1980s have been thoroughly analyzed by *EIR*.[6] After a London or Wall

---

5. A fascinating and detailed account of this debt trap is provided in Rosa Luxemburg's 1913 book, *The Accumulation of Capital*, in Section Three, Chapter 30, "International Loans."

6. "Bankers' Math vs. Human Math: Do You Know How To Count?" on the Brazil debt crisis 1980-90, by Dennis Small, *EIR*, March 19,

Street speculator's initial attack on the currency or financial markets of a nation, the IMF enters the scene, prepared to "bail out" the nation by offering new loans. Accompanying these loans, however, are a set of conditions, such as the forced devaluation of the borrowing nation's currency, increasing its exports—often of primary raw materials and agricultural products, cutting government financing of infrastructure and scientific projects, healthcare and education of its people, and other austerity measures to cut costs and "balance the budget." At the end of each such round of "structural adjustment" by the IMF and the World Bank, the debt levels of the victim country have most often increased rather than decreased, forcing more borrowing with more draconian austerity measures, such as the state being forced to sell its assets, whether they are productive enterprises or natural resources, to foreign companies. Furthermore, governments that resist either the initial attack on their economy or the later intervention by the IMF/World Bank, become subject to defamation campaigns in the media, followed by political destabilization through color revolution, and, in the worst cases, by political or military coups, and even assassinations.

Xinhua/Rouelle Umali

Philippine President Rodrigo Duterte (center) at the groundbreaking ceremony of two China-funded bridges across the Pasig River in Manila, the Philippines, July 17, 2018.

Returning to the China 'Debt-Trap' Narrative

One amazing aspect of the false narrative of China's "debt-trap diplomacy" is the utter lack of any evidence supporting the claims of the authors in these media and academic reports; none of them stand up to serious scrutiny.

What the facts show, is quite contrary to the "impression" intended by much of the anti-Chinese reporting. For example, well-documented research by the China Africa Research Initiative at the School of Advanced International Studies (SAIS-CARI) at Johns Hopkins University, reveals that the majority of African debt is not even held by China, but by trans-Atlantic powers and such Western-backed institutions as the IMF and World Bank.

In its white paper on the upcoming, September meeting of the Forum on China-Africa Cooperation (FOCAC) in Beijing, SAIS-CARI reports, as its first finding, that "Chinese loans are not currently a major contributor to debt distress in Africa. Yet many countries have borrowed heavily from China and others. Any new FOCAC loan pledges will likely take Africa's growing debt burden into account." The white paper reports $133 billion in Chinese loan commitments to Africa over the period 2000-2016, with a very large $30 billion in 2016 following the 2015 FOCAC meeting in Johannesburg. While many African nations have Chinese debt, there are only three nations—Djibouti, Republic of Congo, and Zambia—for which Chinese loans are the most significant contributor to their debt risk. In Cameroon, the African nation ranked fourth in Chinese debt as a portion of total debt, China holds less than one-third of its total debt.

As verified by the authors of this article in the referenced Schiller Institute Special Report, *Extending the New Silk Road to West Asia and Africa*, China's loans and total foreign direct investments (FDI) in Africa are smaller than those of other international institutions, but they are more directed towards construction of infrastructure, manufacturing and agriculture, while investments by American and European companies are directed towards mining and financial services.

China has also emerged as one of the leading sources of aid to African nations and their leading research partner in the fields of agriculture and healthcare. And China has financed many development projects in Africa and

---

1999 and "How the IMF's Policies Destroy the Physical Economy of Nations," covering the Mexican crisis, *EIR*, March 19, 1995.

Southeast Asia through grants, rather than loans. In one very recent case, in July of this year, the groundbreaking ceremony for two new bridges in the Philippines, the Binondo-Intramuros and Estrella-Pantaleon bridges, which are both financed and being built by China, was used by the mass media to arouse alarm and panic about China entrapping the Philippines in a debt trap. During the ceremony, which was attended by President Rodrigo Duterte himself, Chinese Ambassador to the Philippines Zhao Jianhua refuted that notion: "Let me make it quite clear: These projects, these two bridges, are going to be financed by Chinese grants. That is, we're going to build it for free." He added that "actually, there has never been a debt trap. It's all based on mutual agreement," stressing that China never asked for "even one square of real estate in this country." He added that the Philippine government "will own all those projects. So there will be no question of putting yourself in debt. I think your economic team is smart enough."

Industrialization Staircase: Whither the U.S. and Europe?

The tension arising in response to the Belt and Road Initiative and the new paradigm in international relations is not justified. It is entirely due to misconceptions about economics and power relations among nations, that the United States and many nations in the EU have allowed themselves to be herded into negative attitudes towards the BRI. The situation can be likened to a narrow staircase, representing industrialization, with China and the developing sector nations walking upwards. The United States and the EU are on their way down in the direction of deindustrialization. The two reach a point where they meet face to face in the middle of the staircase, blocking the way for each other. This is where the tension rises. It is here that one side must decide to join the other by moving in the same direction, making it easier for both sides to move freely. It would furthermore be beneficial for both sides to make the staircase wider to accommodate everyone, or as President Xi says in describing China's development policy, "making the cake [of economic growth] bigger" so everyone can have a fair share, rather than fighting over a small cake.

The only rational path for the United States and Europe to take is the one outlined most clearly, and for a long time, by Lyndon LaRouche and Helga-Zepp LaRouche, that is, to join the new paradigm of economic, industrial development, best exemplified by the BRI. In light of this, the Schiller Institute, under the leadership of Helga Zepp-LaRouche, has launched an urgent international petition drive, seeking a conference of the United States, Russia, China, and India, to establish a new fixed exchange rate system for world trade and development, modeled on Franklin Roosevelt's concept of the Bretton Woods system. This "new Bretton Woods system" would be the right context for these forces joining hands in the BRI to solve the many economic, social and political problems that have engulfed large parts of the world in the past years, including saving the very economies of the United States and the EU countries themselves.

AN ONGOING DISCUSSION

Will Pakistan Choose the Belt and Road Or Debt Slavery?

by Hussein Askary

Sept. 1—One very pressing and clear example of how a country can today be destroyed by debt, and can be saved from this trap by China, is Pakistan. In Chapter 4 of his "Debtbook Diplomacy" study attacking China for the State Department (see accompanying article), Sam Parker states, under the title "U.S. Interests at Stake," the clear imperialist tendency he subconsciously harbors. Parker's "point 1" states that "China's expanding regional influence and access to South Asian and Pacific Island ports has the long-term potential to alter the regional balance of power away from *effective U.S. naval dominance*" (emphasis added). Worse is to come in point 2: "China's loans undermine the U.S.' ability to *use its own economic assistance to promote U.S. security objectives*. This assistance has provided the U.S. a powerful means to advance its nuclear security and counterterrorism interests in Pakistan" (emphasis added).

Pakistan, for reasons too complex to be sufficiently explained in this article, became a conduit for the Anglo-American geopolitical practice of pitting so-called Islamic forces against the Soviet Union and Russia in the Afghan War that extended from 1979 to 1989, and for the emergence of so-called Islamic jihadist terrorism as a consequence. Pakistan itself became a direct victim of such terrorism.

In that process, Pakistan's economic development plans were halted, and the country became more and more dependent on U.S., British and Saudi financial "assistance," later combined with IMF and World Bank loans.

Today, the Paris Club of lenders (composed almost entirely of Western countries), and multilateral lenders, spearheaded by the IMF and international commercial banks, are Pakistan's largest creditors, not China, according to official statistics provided by the State Bank of Pakistan . Pakistan's foreign debt is expected to surpass $95 billion this year, and debt service is projected to reach $31 billion by 2022-2023. In the current fiscal year, Pakistan will pay $4.2 billion to these foreign creditors. Debt servicing of China-Pakistan Economic Corridor (CPEC) loans will start this year too, but amounts to less than $80 million in repayments, according to the Pakistani daily *Dawn*.

In light of this, it is quite ironic that U.S. Secretary of State Mike Pompeo, the head of the U.S. institution that commissioned Parker's report, warned in July of this year that the U.S. will put pressure on the IMF when it considers a $12 billion bailout package requested earlier this year by the government of Pakistan. "Make no mistake. We will be watching what the IMF does," Pompeo said in an interview with CNBC TV on July 30. "There's no rationale for IMF tax dollars—and associated with that, American dollars that are part of the IMF funding—for those to go to bail out Chinese bondholders or China itself," Pompeo said.

The IMF, and consequently the Paris Club members, have been actively meddling in Pakistan's fiscal policies and its sovereignty through debt rescheduling programs and the conditionalities attached to IMF loans through the Extended Fund Facility, for example. The last such facility included a loan of $6.4 billion in 2016. The conditionalities attached to this kind of loan include, for instance, a government fiscal deficit limit of 4.2%, meaning that any substantial state-backed investments in infrastructure would be impossible. In addition, these conditionalities included the slashing of 200 billion Pakistani rupees (approximately $1.6 billion) from Pakistan's own development plans. It is evident, as in every other IMF/World Bank "bailout package," that the debt grows bigger, and the economy declines further, after these measures are taken.

Pakistan's Growing Debt

Pakistan's growing foreign debt is a direct result of its giant trade deficit, due to the IMF model. Pakistan has been running a yearly deficit of over $23 billion for the past few years, and it is increasing dramatically. Pakistan's main export items are raw materials and staple foodstuffs, and its main manufactured export is textiles. Staple food and raw materials suffer from price oscillations, while the textile sector is not competitive because of Pakistan's collapsing energy supply. And it is exactly the energy sector, together with transportation, that is the main focus of Chinese investments in the CPEC.

In the fiscal year 2017-2018, the trade deficit reached a new record, $37.64 billion. Once again, imports were heavily dominated by oil and gas, amounting to $14.43 billion.

It is obvious that Pakistan's power sector is the most critical element in resolving the country's financial and economic crisis. The total installed capacity for the electricity sector in the country is 25,000 MW (2017) with the average demand being 19,000 MW. The fuel sources are: (1) oil and gas: 14,635 MW, or 64.2% of total power generation; (2) hydropower: 6,611 MW or 29% of total generating capacity; and (3) nuclear power: 1,322 MW or 5.8% of the total generating capacity. Bear in mind that the cost of importing oil and gas is about $13-14 billion annually.

The CPEC's energy production component, the main focus of China-Pakistan cooperation, can ensure the generation of enough electricity to eliminate the deficit in electricity supplies and prepare the economy for a further surge in industrial activity. The breakdown of the investments that are completed, under construction, or in negotiation is as follows: coal plants: 8,580 MW; hydropower: 2,700 MW; other thermal plants (natural gas): 825 MW; solar power plants: 900 MW; wind farms: 350 MW. The expected total new electricity generating capacity is 13,355 MW.

The total cost of all these power generation projects (including mining of coal and electricity transmission lines) is estimated to be $23-30 billion, which is approximately the cost of two years' imports of oil and gas, and less than half the annual trade deficit.

Which Road Will Pakistan Take?

In his election victory speech of July 26, 2018, Pakistani Prime Minister-elect Imran Khan focused on the economic crisis engulfing the country and pledged to continue cooperation with China on the CPEC. "Our economic crisis is such that we want to have good relations with all our neighbors.... China gives us a huge opportunity through CPEC, to use it to drive investment into Pakistan. We want to learn from China how they brought 700 million people out of poverty." Addressing the U.S. policy, Khan said: "With the U.S., we want to have a mutually beneficial relationship.... Up until now, that has been one-way. The U.S. thinks it gives us aid to fight their war." As for the chronic, British-orchestrated conflict between India and Pakistan, especially the dispute over Kashmir, Khan said: "I think it will be very good for all of us if we have good relations with India. We need to have trade ties, and the more we will trade, both countries will benefit.... Pakistan's and India's leadership should sit at a table and try to fix this problem. It's not going anywhere."

Interestingly, both Pakistan and India became full members in the Shanghai Cooperation Organization during the June 2018 summit in Qingdao, China, raising hopes that within this new context of the new paradigm, tensions between Pakistan and India, stoked for decades by British influence, can at last be resolved. This will be a necessary condition for finally solving the permanent war situation in Afghanistan.

For Pakistan to overcome its debt crisis, it first needs to resolve its trade deficit. To do that, it needs to raise the productivity of its economy. Without ample supply of electricity, transport and efficient logistics, this task will be impossible. The Western loans to Pakistan are merely filling holes in the budget without freeing any resources for resolving the core problems.

Political and social unrest, as a consequence of this situation, will make it impossible for any government to hold the country together and achieve stability and growth. The very security of society and the government itself will be at risk, if this situation is not resolved quickly. The CPEC is right now the only concrete, constructive, and available remedy for this apparently insurmountable dilemma. Without increasing the productivity of the Pakistani economy as a whole, there will be no way out of the crisis. The CPEC provides a great opportunity for Pakistan's development, if Pakistan's leadership will take advantage of it.

Pakistan, which does have an industrial base, a relatively well-educated and young labor force, and international business connections through the Pakistani diaspora all around the world, can easily overcome its trade deficit and foreign debt burden in the foreseeable future.

November 24, 2008

TODAY'S GLOBAL CRISIS

The Truth of Bretton Woods Lies Within Physical Science

by Lyndon H. LaRouche, Jr.

As I had forecast, at the close of July 2007, the world as a whole had entered a great financial-economic break-down-crisis. Yet, even after sixteen months of this crisis, few among the leading figures of contemporary Europe, have shown any relevant comprehension of what are still, for today's policy-shaping, the strategically crucial features of that specific period of actual history of Europe since the seminal interval between the 1890 ouster of Germany's Chancellor Otto von Bismarck and the 1901 assassination of U.S. President William McKinley.[1] For that and related reasons, few leading economists and other prominent political figures in Europe, or elsewhere, today, retain any competent knowledge of those bitterly fought issues between U.S. President Franklin Roosevelt and the British imperialist system, since the time of President Roosevelt's first Presidential campaign of 1932. Thus, true knowledge of the meaning of "Bretton Woods" virtually died out about the time of the deaths of the Fifth Republic's President Charles de Gaulle and his relevant German collaborator, Chancellor Konrad Adenauer.

So, recently, a 2008 event organized in Modena, Italy, produced what was falsely alleged there to have been the principle employed by U.S. President Franklin D. Roosevelt in defining the principle of a Bretton Woods System, during his 1944 conference.*

*Contrary to the baseless views prevalent at that Modena affair, what President Roosevelt had actually proposed was, in all essential features, an **anti-British-imperialist, anti-monetarist** system. His proposed system excluded any defense of that British empire's predatory interest. The British imperial interest was that which had been presented to that same Bretton Woods conference by President Roosevelt's adversary of that occasion, the same pro-fascist British banker John Maynard Keynes, that of Keynes' 1937 Berlin edition of his **General Theory**.*

What was resolved at Modena was, sadly, a pilot-design for a global disaster. It was an inherently failed scheme adopted in an effort to lure influential Russian figures whose ignorance of the actual issues of 1944 Bretton Woods was being exploited by certain swindlers known to me, swindlers who were playing a cata-

---

1. The ouster of Bismarck, the assassination of President Sadi Carnot of France, the Dreyfus case, the British Royal family's launching of Japan against China, Fashoda, and the assassination of President McKinley: these events of 1890-1901 set the stage for the 1905-1914, British launching of what became known as "geopolitical" World War I, which became, in turn, the 1922 launching of fascism and the road into World War II. These dates are not particular, Cartesian events; rather, these apparent events are symptomatic expressions of *a dynamic (e.g., Leibnizian-Riemannian) form of process of unfolding phase-shifts in global warfare,* conducted by the Anglo-Dutch Liberal empire, leading from 1890 into the presently ongoing, global breakdown-crisis of the present year-end.

---

* Among the participants in this conference was a small group of former associates of Lyndon LaRouche, who had deserted the LaRouche movement to join the British camp. Over the last year or two of the writing of this document, these LaRouche renegades pulled Russian, Italian, and other participants into a series of conferences, including the one in July 2008 in Modena, Italy, duping them into discussing a phony New Bretton Woods, along the same Keynesian, anti-Roosevelt lines more recently specified by British Prime Minister Gordon Brown.

President Franklin D. Roosevelt with Treasury Secretary Henry Morgenthau, Jr. (left) in 1934. Morgenthau represented FDR's policy for the Bretton Woods system, in opposition to the British pro-fascist banker John Maynard Keynes.

wide, the leading economist in the defense of the actual policy proposed by President Franklin Roosevelt at the 1944 Bretton Woods conference. Opposite to that, the ill-informed scheme presented at Modena, had the makings of what could have become a great tragedy, not only for Russia itself, but the world generally.[2]

There has been a decent minority of professional economists who have had certain competencies within their limited field of work, but even those have failed, and that systemically, in the larger field of my own special competence, the physical science of long-range economic forecasting. In fact, France's Jacques Cheminade and I had been the only professional economists, internationally, to date, who have expressed an actual grasp of the essential significance of President Franklin Roosevelt's 1944 reform. The contrary view expressed by Modena 2008 was essentially a hoax foisted upon those credulous persons who had been misled by witting swindlers, misled into failing to consult the readily available, only competent authorities on the subject of Bretton Woods today. I had been the authority who, uniquely, introduced the Bretton Woods policy to the Parliament of Italy during earlier years. What the two scamps produced, fraudulently, in my name, was not merely a hoax, but implicitly a deadly one for any government duped into adopting the erroneous view of the matter presented in the resolutions reached at that conference.

The essence of the model folly unleashed at Modena, is, simply, the fact, that the Modena resolution was a

lytic role within the organizing of the Modena affair. Essentially, as a result of the clear case of their ignorance of the relevant history of the matter, the participants in the Modena conference were lured into a potentially fatal, Keynesian trap.

As a matter of currently notable historical ironies, Josef Stalin of 1944-1946 had been wiser. Now, a folly similar to that of Modena has been organized in Brazil, this time under the open direction of the international, British drug-trafficking interests deployed into Brazil.

The motive behind the earlier attempted swindle of Russian and other participants at that Modena conference, had relatively deep roots in a frankly Fabian, fascist, post-World War II plot, a morally and culturally depraved "Cold War" plot known as the Congress for Cultural Freedom (CCF). The root of that particular, 2008 swindle attempted at Modena itself, is to be traced to events of nearly forty years earlier, in August-September 1971, when I had emerged suddenly as the one who was to be recognized as the only known economist who had repeatedly forewarned economist and related circles in the U.S.A. of that probable, early breakdown of the Bretton Woods system which had just occurred in August 1971. Since that time, I have remained, world

---

2. The conspirators in this hoax included two scoundrels who had fled from my own international association in response to my intention to pursue serious charges against their scheme's principal associate. The way that figure's cronies jumped ship, when I was about to press those charges, should remind us of François Rabelais's case of "the sheep of Panurge." The use of the pair of scoundrels notable for their role at Modena, is a typical echo of the dirty methods specific to such veterans of the Congress for Cultural Freedom as John Train and his Fabian friends from the ranks of the Tony Blair ministry.

foredoomed catastrophe based upon mere monetarists' presumptions. Whereas, President Franklin Roosevelt's design was based on a Hamiltonian credit-system, rather than the implicitly pro-fascist, British imperialist system of mere monetarist Keynes.

Bretton Woods Today

The presently relevant aspects of the history of the actual Bretton Woods issue since a relevant August-December 1971 turning-point, have been, summarily, the following.

From August 15, 1971 on, I had challenged all of those academic economists of the U.S.A., who had previously repeatedly rejected my standing forecast of such an apocalyptic event. After that event had occurred, I had challenged them to reply to my charge, that the monetary events of August 1971 showed that they had acted as hardened "quackademics" in their foolish insistence that "the built-in stabilizers" would prevent any possible breakdown of the then present Anglo-American monetary system. Months after I had condemned those failed economists on this point, my repeated, well documented insistence on that point had driven the pained "quackademics" to the point they moved to select their champion to meet my challenge. Therefore, the putatively leading Keynesian economist Abba Lerner, had been recently brought from London to assume the status of a "super-professor," at a New York university campus, where he was chosen to defend the flawed American academic economists generally against my standing charges.[3]

Thus, near the close of 1971, shortly after I had defeated the chosen Fabian advocate of the Congress for Cultural Freedom, Professor Abba Lerner, in the then celebrated debate at New York's Queens College, I received news of a threat against me from that Congress's spokesman. The threat from that spokesman, Professor Sidney Hook, was: **Your champion has defeated our champion (Lerner), but we shall cause your man to be blacklisted, forever, from every public forum, permanently, for what he has done.**

Notably, the issue which resulted in Professor Lerner's exposing himself, fatally, in the matter of that debate, was Lerner's voluntary defense, on that occasion, of the policies of the Hjalmar Schacht who had been the Bank of England's special asset in bringing Adolf Hitler into power in Germany. This sympathy for Hitler's Schacht, as expressed by Lerner, was an echo of both Schacht himself, and of Keynes' 1937 apology for the economic methods of Nazism, Keynes' **General Theory.**[4]

The "we" of Professor Hook's threat against me proved to include another notorious international figure of that same "Congress for Cultural Freedom (CCF)," "Cold War" veteran and banker John Train. Hook and Lerner are now long deceased, but, at last report, Train is not. The very Congress for Cultural Freedom itself had seemed, finally, to have passed away (formally) with the fall of the Berlin Wall, but Train's active role in this affair against me, so to speak, rolls on, deploying his gutter-scum, typified by wretches such as assets in Train Dennis King and John Foster "Chip" Berlet, and by elements drawn, liberally, from former British Prime Minister Tony Blair's circles, still today.[5]

Back more than sixty years ago, the actual target of that same faction's hatred, then, had been U.S. President Franklin Delano Roosevelt and Roosevelt's followers within associations such as the war-time Office of Strategic Services (OSS). To the best of my knowledge, the post-war leaders from OSS chief General Donovan's faction, such as one-time CIA chief Bill Casey, who had been part of OSS, have died out over the course of the 1980s and early 1990s; but, some post-war recruits to those intelligence circles from a younger generation, who had been adopted by "Donovan's boys" later on, have been active, under other auspices, still today. In spirit and tradition, those of us who were, or became later a part of this specific heritage of President Franklin Roosevelt's Presidency, look back to such Nineteenth Century "birth-right" leaders of the Society of the Cincinnati as James Fenimore Cooper. War in defense of that U.S.A., by such patriots among us, goes on, thus, still today.[6]

---

3. The term "quackademics" was minted and circulated by me, then, for that occasion.

4. It must be recalled, that in 1937 the leading British Liberals of that time were, as King Edward VIII had been, deeply involved in support of the Adolf Hitler project in Germany.

5. Train assumed a visibly leading position in the covert operations against me personally shortly after President Ronald Reagan's televised presentation of the Strategic Defense Initiative (SDI). Train was, in fact, involved in every principal, covert, legal and related operation against me into 1989, and has continued that same activity up to most recent report on the matter received.

6. This is typical of U.S. patriots recruited to such private, patriotic associations. In my own case, my earliest U.S. antecedents are dated to the

EIRNS/Laurence Hecht   Library of Congress

Gen. William Donovan (right), the head of the war-time Office of Strategic Services, was a partisan of President Roosevelt in battles against not only the Nazis, but their "former" supporters in Britain and the United States. OSS veteran William Casey (left), who headed the CIA from 1981 to 1987, was a leader of Donovan's faction of patriots in the intelligence community. Younger members of this grouping remain active today.

Sometimes, as now, defending that U.S. legacy against London's Wall Street gang, means smoking out the present heirs of those pre-1942 Anglo-American and other one-time backers of the rise of Adolf Hitler, such as the grandfather of U.S. President George W. Bush, Jr., the Prescott Bush who typifies those who had changed their political trade-marks, but not their inner character, when the Nazi fortunes had changed with the entry of President Franklin Roosevelt's U.S.A. into that war. The same pro-Hitler gang typified by Brown Brothers Harriman then, lives on, if under new banners, still today, as the same organization operating under what passes now for a "respectable, conservative" cover. All

of my own personal adversaries of any relevant, weighty significance, are drawn from precisely those offshoots, such as President George W. Bush, Jr., of what had been the Wall-Street-linked fascist sympathizers of Mussolini and Hitler from back then.[7]

Now, a menaced humanity must win that war against those British and American-Tory interests descended from such as Judge Lowell and the traitor Aaron Burr who founded the Bank of Manhattan. If we do not, the presently ongoing lurch into a threatened, planet-wide "New Dark Age," will soon virtually eliminate each and all among the contending parties throughout this planet. To understand the two Bush U.S. Presidents and their role in this ugly present reality, one must remember who and what Prescott Bush of Brown Brothers Harriman had really been, back when Adolf Hitler was enjoying the backing of the British monarchy, of the Bank of England's Montagu Norman, and of Winston Churchill, too.

Once you abandon that popular delusion which denied the essential fact, that Adolf Hitler and his role had been that of an originally British creation, top-down, rather than a specifically German one; and, once you take into account former German Chancellor Bismarck's prophetic warning, that Prince of Wales Edward Albert's motive for causing the firing of Bismarck by the incredibly foolish Wilhelm II, had been an intended replay of the Seven Years War, you were on the way to understanding how the Anglo-Dutch Liberal empire of Paolo Sarpi's descendants, has been playing virtually all of the nations of continental Europe, as if each dupe were fish for the catching, most of the time, most among them still dupes up through the present minute I write this report.

Thus, today's strategic reality behind the scandalous features of what might appear to some to be the relatively obscure Modena event, is as follows.

U.S.A. and Quebec of the first half of the Sixteenth Century, those settlers who had defended their adopted America as patriots should, especially since their revolt against the 1763 launching of imperial oppression by the imperial British East India Company of Lord Shelburne et al. Adam Smith, personally a creature of Lord Shelburne, represents British imperialist dogma in economics to the present day. Opposing Smith et al., the Society of the Cincinnati is a typical case of such "sons and daughters of the American Revolution" who recognized Adam Smith as an embodiment of the enemy of civilization in his time. Since that same development of 1763, the enemies from within the U.S.A. have been centered around the Wall Street gang's role as a continuation of those "American Tories" associated with the British East India Company's Judge Lowell. Cf. Anton Chaitkin, ***Treason in America*** EPUB Kindle PDF (New York: New Benjamin Franklin House, 1985).

7. Their names are "Legion," and include all of the principal sources of legal and major press harassment, since the early 1970s, to the present day, on both sides of the Atlantic.

Introduction:
What Is This Brutish Empire?

To those who, in science as in war, gave a full measure of their devotion.

I say again, as in relevant earlier locations, that the subject with which any political report on this matter of the Brutish Empire should begin today, is that of the strategic role played by the Venetian marriage-counselor of England's King Henry VIII, Francesco Zorzi,[8] a role which led to that division of Europe, between its northern and Mediterranean coastal settlements, which has continued to dominate the long wave of global developments, since 1689-1763, as in the present outbreak of an existential form of global strategic crisis.

As I have already emphasized this point in locations published earlier, the Venetian faction behind the religious warfare of 1492-1648 Europe, had split, meanwhile, into two parts, following the Council of Trent. Out of this, the followers of the Servite monk Paolo Sarpi emerged as relatively triumphant, in the guise of a predominantly Protestant current, a current based, chiefly, away from the Mediterranean maritime bases, into bases along the coasts of northern Europe. The relatively victorious party led by Sarpi, was characterized by its shift from the Aristotelean tradition maintained by the Mediterranean-based faction, to the rabid irrationalism of the medieval William of Ockham. Ockham's irrationalist faction became known, for that reason, as expressing the reductionist dogma of modern Anglo-Dutch Liberalism (i.e., empiricism, positivism).[9]

Thus, since that interval, the dominant role of the Anglo-Dutch Liberal oligarchies arrayed along Europe's Northern coastlines, has been countered, in effect, by the division of the English-speaking powers of the world between the essentially usurious, Anglo-Dutch Liberal financier oligarchy (the so-called "free trade" party) and the so-called "protectionist" spirit of the American patriotic faction. All major wars in the world since that February 1763 outcome known as the "Peace of Paris" which concluded the so-called "Seven Years War," and included the Napoleonic wars, have been radiated reflections of the essentially existential conflict between the already emerging American System of 1620-1763 and the Anglo-Dutch Liberalism of the period since the 1688-89 role of William of Orange.[10]

That crucial feature of all modern world history since the turbulent transition, from Stuart to Orange, of 1688-89 England, was echoed, for today's reference, in a celebrated remark by (then) former German Chancellor Otto von Bismarck, who emphasized that the motive behind what was to become known widely as "World War I," was the British monarchy's intention to ruin continental Europe through a new "Seven Years War." The British imperialist faction of that time was already referring to that 1763 tradition which would come to be identified, later, following President Abraham Lincoln's defeat of Lord Palmerston's effort to break up the U.S. Union, as "geopolitics."[11]

That crucial, February 1763 Peace of Paris, has two principal implications for reading the implications of the presently onrushing, global breakdown-crisis of the present world monetarist system.

The first implication, which would tend to be understood more easily, is that Britain's strategic policy since the Dutch role in orchestrating the self-inflicted ruin of French "Sun King" Louis XIV, had been to ruin all durable challenges to the intentions of Paolo Sarpi's Anglo-Dutch imperialist followers, through orchestrating new applications of the strategy of the Seven Years War. That ruin had been done to prevent any effective challenge to Anglo-Dutch imperialism from within the continent of Europe. The way in which the London of Jeremy Bentham's British Foreign Office played the unsuspecting, virtual puppet-emperor Napoleon I at that time, is an illustration of the point, as is also the case of the rise and fall of the British policeman who came to be called Napoleon III. World Wars I and II, later, were organized by the British Foreign Office in the same mode.

The second implication, rarely understood by out-

---

8. Pronounced, and spelled, in England, as "Giorgi."

9. I.e., "de-constructionist."

10. Cf. H. Graham Lowry, ***How the Nation Was Won: America's Untold Story*** EPUB Kindle PDF (Washington, D.C.: Executive Intelligence Review, 1988). For a brief period, during the reign of England's Queen Anne, Gottfried Leibniz played a leading role in turning the history of Europe in a better direction.

11. The most notable issue behind British "geopolitics," was the threat to British imperial maritime supremacy from the development of the transcontinental railway system in the U.S.A., and its echo in the similar developments within continental Eurasia.

German Chancellor Otto von Bismarck (left) was ousted in 1890, thanks to pressure from Britain's Prince of Wales Edward Albert (shown, right, as King Edward VII). Bismarck warned that the British intended a replay of the Seven Years War, to destroy continental Europe. It happened, with the outbreak of World War I in 1914.

siders, even among insiders who have been high-ranking in governments, or in academic political science, is the following.

The essence of the British empire, while apparently territorial in its included effect, is not really the empire of a nation-state (e.g., the United Kingdom), but is, actually, primarily, a continuation of that financier-imperial, monetary system of the Venice which emerged as an independent imperial power through hegemony over the financial affairs of Europe (and beyond) since about 1,000 A.D. Empires have come and passed, but, until now, like the legendary Phoenix, new empires have arisen, not autochthonously, but from the very ashes of the fallen predecessor. So, for example, today, the Anglo-Dutch Liberal swindle known as the combined dynamic of "globalization" and the fascist "environmentalism" of both Britain's Duke of Edinburgh and Philip's late accomplice and Nazi-SS veteran Prince Bernhard of the Netherlands, is essentially a cloak for the actual imperial, monetarist system of international finance, so-called "free trade," which is the heritage of the Ockhamite Liberalism established by the faction of Paolo Sarpi.

Leibniz & the American System

In the longer skein of American history, the essential difference in philosophy and government, between the founding American patriots and their immediate British adversaries, has been the American patriots' ad-

herence to the legacy of Gottfried Leibniz, whereas the British and their co-thinkers in North America and Brazil are, systemically, followers of the pro-slavery John Locke. This philosophical difference was the crucial issue of law between U.S. patriots and the racist scoundrels of the Confederacy. The latter insisted on basing their constitution of the Confederacy on the perverted John Locke, whereas the 1776 U.S. Declaration of Independence based itself on the specifically anti-Locke "pursuit of happiness," as this concept had been taken from Leibniz's *New Essay's* rebuttal of Locke. Leibniz's attack on Locke, as it was quoted to crucial effect in the U.S. Declaration of Independence, was the central point of reference for the members of the circle of Benjamin Franklin who crafted the ***U.S. Declaration of Independence***. The same Leibnizian principle is the cornerstone of ***The Constitution of the United States***, as presented in the Constitution's statement of intention of constitutional principle, its Preamble.

The difficulty which many present-day, post-1968 European political figures suffer in their customarily failed, recent-times' efforts to explain away the U.S. constitutional system, is that the European systems, to the extent they are still presently corrupted by the influence of British ideology itself, or as the relics of the Habsburg legacy, are premised on an axiomatically imperialist conception of society and of the nature of the human individual soul. *The essence of this pro-oligarchical element of corruption in European culture, is ex-*

While John Locke called happiness "the utmost pleasure we are capable of," Gottfried Wilhelm Leibniz (shown here) insisted that "true happiness ought always to be the object of our desires. . . . The less desire is guided by reason, the more it tends to present pleasure and not to happiness, that is to say, to lasting pleasure." Leibniz's conception of "life, liberty, and the pursuit of happiness" was adopted by the U.S. Declaration of Independence—contrary to almost ubiquitous lies by historians that Locke was the "father" of the Declaration.

John Locke, whose 1669 Constitution for the Government of Carolina codified slavery, wrote elsewhere: "The great and chief end . . . of men uniting into commonwealths, and putting themselves under government, is the preservation of their Property." Slaves "cannot in that state be considered as any part of civil society, the chief end whereof is the preservation of property." Those who wanted Locke's "life, liberty, and property" to be included in the Declaration of Independence, lost out to the Leibnizians.

pressed most clearly in the European habit of preference for what are, in fact, imperialist monetary systems, rather than a credit-system, such as the principle of a credit-system which inheres as a principle of government and natural law in the design of the U.S. Declaration of Independence and Federal Constitution.

The defective element met in European traditions of today, relative to the implications of the origins and crafting of the U.S. Federal constitutional system, is expressed most concisely in *the idea of monetary systems*. In ancient through modern history at large, this element is not a specifically European, but, rather, a Eurasian tendency, rooted in such examples as the monetarist roots of the decline and fall of Sumer and other west Asian systems, and in that specific fusion of such Asian and emerging European imperialist systems following the decline of Greece in the Peloponnesian War. For precisely such reasons, Plato's principal target for eradication in his plan for the redemption of Athens from the Sophists' folly underlying the Peloponnesian War, was the cult of Delphi, a crucial center

of monetarist and related forms of depraved, implicitly Satanic practices.[12] It should be the target for any fully witting promoter of civilized forms of life on this planet for today.

Here lies the essential, principled issue of President Franklin Roosevelt's systemic opposition to that intrinsically imperialist system of monetarism defended, and promoted by John Maynard Keynes.

----

12. The site of Delphi includes adjoining small "temples" of usury, each representing the monetary interest of a corresponding Greek city. The road down from the site reaches to a port, and into the Mediterranean markets for the practice of usury and kindred abominations. European cultures were rooted in maritime traditions and modalities. Modern European imperialism since the time of Plato, has been a blending of models of Asian imperialisms with European maritime authorities, forming thus into a single imperialist form of "oligarchical model," from the ancient Roman Empire, Byzantium, the Venetian-Norman systems, and British imperialism today. Hence, the characteristic of British imperialism, and British imperialism's organization of what became known as Prince Edward Albert's design for "World War I," as British imperialism's reaction against the victory of President Lincoln over Lord Palmerston's Confederacy puppets.

1. The Myth Called Money

In beginning this present chapter of the report, I present a set of illustrations for the purpose of identifying some of the terrain I shall examine in a more rigorous way, either later in this same chapter, or later in this report.

Begin the following points of illustration with samplings from the experience of studies of some features of the presently defunct Soviet economy.

The common intellectual root of recurring ruin of the recent century's trans-Atlantic and Russian economies, has been the influence of the characteristically Sarpian dogma of Adam Smith, an influence from which both western Liberal economies and the Marxian practice of the former Soviet economy have suffered *liberally, and systemically*.[13]

As the effects of presently spiraling, global hyperinflation, or deep economic depression-collapse, should be sufficient to illustrate that point: in reality, *there is no intrinsic value in money as such, other than the usefulness of money as a medium of circulation of those goods and services which do in fact represent the expression of real wealth.* The practical social value of a system of uttering and circulating money, lies in that function, not in the relative money-valuation attributed to the objects which are circulated by aid of a money-system. There is no coincidence between economic value and price, except for pathological ones. Moreover, money-systems usually do circulate many kinds of objects and forms of services which, in fact, contribute no net wealth to society, but, often, as in monopolistic abuse, "recreational" drug-trafficking, prostitution, or forms of gambling such as trafficking in so-called "financial derivatives," represent a purely destructive value for which money has been paid, often at a fool's fantastically exorbitant high price.[14]

A money-system is useful only to the degree that it is very, very modest in putting forward ontological claims. Money must not be considered as defining value; rather, sound notions of relative value must be

PBS

Contrary to Milton Friedman and just about every other economist today, money has no intrinsic value. Its practical social value lies in promoting those goods and services which represent real wealth.

crafted and adopted by society as valuations to be superimposed upon objects which might be bought and sold. "Free trade" is worse than being simply lunacy, and usury is, systemically, a crime against humanity. To restate the point: economic value must be defined according to relevant physical principles of dynamics, that within systems treated as integral wholes. In other words, the only competent basis for a study of relative economic values is Riemannian dynamics.[15]

In any case, economic value for society does not repose in objects as such, but, in even the best of cases, in the effect of their consumption. (Naturally, to be consumable, they must, first, be produced.) What must be measured is the gains in productivity of the society as a whole over time, *gains obtained through consumption of that output, as by the successful application of scientific progress*, that for the cases that the effect of consumption more than offsets the attrition associated with the entropy inherent in continued reliance on any fixed level of scientific technology.

For example: a true wealth effect may be expressed in terms of Academician V.I. Vernadsky's notions of Biosphere and Noösphere: as increase of the Biosphere relative to the abiotic domain, and as increase of the Noösphere relative to the Biosphere, all on the condition that the Biosphere is increased, relative to the abi-

---

13. Once you accept the notion that Adam Smith defines economy, everything else you believe, however correct, or simply innocent in itself, is corrupted by the rot which inheres in the disease of Smith himself.

14. Such financial instruments should be simply outlawed, and thus cancelled in their entirety as they were to be considered as inherently fraudulent transactions.

---

15. I am not suggesting that Riemannian dynamics has been used for this purpose in society so far. I am stating that actual valuations should be a fair approximation of values which could be defined better by aid of Riemannian dynamics.

otic domain, as an expression of the increase of the Noösphere relative to the Biosphere.

Thus, for example, Soviet science tended to prosper, relatively, in its accomplishments in the military field, while Russia was often, at the same time, relatively, a catastrophe in the domain of economic policy otherwise. This irony of the Soviet case was, essentially, that Soviet military and related science was driven by concern for relevant, science-driven technological strategic advantage; whereas, the Soviet economy otherwise tended, culturally, toward technological stagnation or kindred expressions of that incompetence which is inherent in the doctrine adopted by the dupes of Lord Shelburne's toady, Adam Smith, such as Karl Marx. In the domain of economy, the Liberal ideology copied into the writings of Adam Smith, had, wittingly, or not, banned actual science from the practice of economy.[16] No fanatic is more dangerous to humanity than one, like a believer in Adam Smith, who believes fervently in such as paying tribute to such a nothing as the god of money.

In that case, advances in science (i.e., the Noösphere) are gains for society if this apparent gain is accompanied, and thus supported, by relative gains in the Biosphere.

The explanation for that Soviet military exception itself, should be considered to be elementary, in the best sense of the use of the term "elementary." It is the transformation of physical economic output, upwards, through the successful application of discovered principles of physical science (or, their likeness) which is the sole source of net gain (excepting looting, of course) in a physical economy,

So, it must be emphasized, that effective forms of active modern military strategic requirements are rooted, since Niccolo Machiavelli, in the dynamics of Nicholas of Cusa and Leonardo da Vinci, and are science-driven.[17]

In contrast to that, modern economic practice infected with the disease of Adam Smith's hoax tends, axiomatically, toward "zero technological growth," stagnation, and, as in the U.S.A. and western and central Europe today, the verge of an economic breakdown-crisis in the international economy. The science-driver influence associated with World War II continued, although wavering, on both sides, until the 1962 "missiles crisis." The 1963 advent of the first government of Britain's Prime Minister Harold Wilson, signaled the onset of what would become, over decades, a massive, degenerative wrecking of the productive sector of the economy of the United Kingdom. The launching of the U.S. official war in Vietnam, signaled the unleashing of the destruction of the U.S. economy, a trend which had fallen to below a net-zero, physical balance during U.S. fiscal year 1967-68,[18] and fell at an accelerating rate from that time to the present verge of a general breakdown of almost everything, under the present last gasp of the administration of President George W. Bush, Jr., the grandson of the man who had financed Hitler's career at an historically crucial moment.[19]

This fact will be resisted, as it already has been, by those who insist that price is a measure of value, or who count short-term gains as progress, even when the loss from physical-economic decadence and depletion far exceeds the nominal short-term gains perceived through the folly of mere financial-accounting practices. On this

---

16. Adam Smith, *The Theory of the Moral Sentiments*, 1759; *The Wealth of Nations*, 1776.

17. E.g., *The First Ten Books of Livy*; *The Art of War*. Although the concept of dynamics was introduced into modern Europe, by name, by Gottfried Leibniz, it was already, as emphasized by Albert Einstein, the implicit method of Johannes Kepler's *The Harmonies of the World*. That is, a method which Kepler rightly attributed, in fact, to Nicholas of Cusa (e.g, *De Docta Ignorantia*) and to the method adopted, from Cusa, by Leonardo da Vinci. *Dynamics*, by that name, was introduced to modern Europe by Leibniz in his *Dynamica* (1691), his exposure of the hoaxes of Descartes (1692) and his *Specimen Dynamicum* (1695). Dy-

namics is a revival of the ancient principle of *dynamis* of the Pythagoreans and Plato. Modern dynamics, as so defined by Einstein, is intrinsically Keplerian in its core- principle.

18. It is most notable at this point, that it was never accidental that I emerged, repeatedly, as, in point of fact, the most successful long-range economic forecaster over the 1957-2008 interval to date. My forecasts were not based on statistical trends, but trends in relevant aspects of economic policy, especially physical-economic policy. I explain this and its significance below.

19. It must be emphasized that Prescott Bush, the grandfather of President George W. Bush, Jr., was the official of Brown Brothers Harriman who conducted the rescue of Hitler's Nazi Party at a crucial moment. Brown Brothers Harriman, was the private firm associated with the head of the Bank of England, the same Montagu Norman who was the Hitler supporter who had deployed Hjalmar Schacht to launch the economic-financial program required to prepare Hitler's regime for the intended military destruction of Russia. The right-wing financial support for the regime of President George W. Bush, Jr., has been from the present generation of the same Anglo-American social-financial set which had previously supplied Anglo-American backing for Adolf Hitler. Russian leaders, or other continental European leaders, today, who overlook that fact, need their political rear ends kicked.

©*Washington Star* collection,
D.C. Public Library

The Nazi party was liberally supplied with funds by the Bank of England's Gov. Montagu Norman (right) and by Prescott Bush (center) of the New York investment banking house Brown Brothers, Harriman. They worked closely with German Reichsbank chief Hjalmar Schacht (shown on the left, with Hitler). It was only Hitler's "double-cross," in attacking Britain and France in May-June 1940, instead of striking east to Russia, that convinced his disgruntled Anglo-American sympathizers to join the fight against him.

and related accounts, most financial and related forecasting has been not only misleading, but essentially fraudulent as a matter of principle, and that fraudulence has become increasingly willful, especially since the aftermath of the wrecking of the U.S. economy under the post-1976 influence of the David Rockefeller-backed Trilateral Commission.

U.S. President Richard Nixon's *in flagrante* adoption of Adam Smith, converged upon, and was augmented by the neo-malthusian, anti-science ideology often found among the 68er terrorists' ranks, as this decadence was expressed in efforts of that modern Dionysian cult's obsession, in the name "of nature," or the name of "the environment," not only to block, but stamp out, even reverse economic progress in physical science's investments in the increase of the productive powers of labor.[20]

---

20. If "fair is fair," then it were "fair" to pay such modern dionysiacs in kind; since they take pride in producing less than nothing, they deserve a fair share in that less than nothing which their enterprise produces.

Kepler as an Economist

That which I have just summarized, so, is a reasonable explanation; but, it is only a useful explanation. The essential truth of the matter is already located in those relevant Egyptian and Classical Greek antecedents of modern science associated with the names of *Sphaerics* and *dynamis,* as these topics appear in the works of the Pythagoreans and Plato. Those ancient sources' wisdom reappeared in modern science with, principally, the founding of modern science by Cardinal Nicholas of Cusa, as in his seminal ***De Docta Ignorantia***. As Albert Einstein emphasized this fact, all *competent* modern, applied physical science is premised upon the unique accomplishment of Cusa's intellectual heir, Johannes Kepler, in defining the harmonic composition of the Solar system. The corollary is, that a science which rejects, or simply ignores that principle, the principle typified by the work of Kepler, Riemann, and Einstein, is, in that degree, not competent.

Examine these crucially important points more closely. Consider the matters pertaining to the subjects

Library of Congress

Karl Marx denounced the American System economist Henry Carey, later the advisor to President Abraham Lincoln, as a "bourgeois vulgar economist." Marx wrote to Engels in 1852: "That bourgeois society in the United States has not yet developed far enough to make the class struggle obvious and comprehensible is most strikingly proved by H.C. Carey, the only American economist of importance." Carey was the author of The Harmony of Interests, *the exposition of the American System, in opposition to "class struggle." Marx, perhaps unwittingly, was a follower of Venice's Paolo Sarpi and a tool of Britain's Lord Palmerston.*

of *Kepler, Sarpi,* and *The Protestant Ethic.*

As I have stressed in other locations, competent modern Europeans science was launched through the leading influence of two outstanding, seminal figures arising from the wreckage of a preceding Fourteenth Century, European "new dark age": Filippo Brunelleschi (1377-1446), and, more significantly, Nicholas of Cusa (1401-1464).

Brunelleschi's manifold, true significance was expressed most precisely in the case of his use of the principle of the catenary as the unique physical principle, without which the construction of the cupola of Santa Maria del Fiore would not have been possible at that time. This notion of the catenary, which was not adequately grasped until the work of Gottfried Leibniz in defining the principle of universal least action, had already appeared, nonetheless, as an important principle of physics, after Brunelleschi, in some work of Leonardo da Vinci. Since the fraud by Galileo on this subject, later, has been made clear, one can be confident that Leibniz's discovery of the concept of a universal physical principle of least action, in this matter, also demonstrates the quality of the mind of Brunelleschi shown by use of the catenary for the construction of the cupola.

Otherwise, Nicholas of Cusa, with his avowed followers such as Leonardo da Vinci and Johannes Kepler, is outstanding as the greatest genius of his century, not only for what he accomplished then, but in respect to

the consequences of his work for centuries to come thereafter, to the present day.

I emphasize these just stated considerations here, because they go to the heart of the issues to be exposed as the prevalent, politically motivated, empiricist and kindred, deconstructionist frauds which have been deployed in the name of physical science today. I mean, most emphatically, the fraud of liberalism introduced, by Paolo Sarpi, as what became the universal hallmark of British (i.e., Anglo-Dutch Liberal) imperialism, globally, still today. It is these frauds which must be examined, if one is to locate the source for the incompetence, of British influence on the U.S.A. and continental Europe, which, chiefly, has led the world as a whole to the verge of a presently onrushing general breakdown-crisis of the entire world's economy now.

To come directly to the crucial point at hand: the brand of so-called "science" associated with worship of Isaac Newton, is not to be treated as science, but, rather, as a very nasty sort of pagan religion, called "Liberalism." It is only after we have considered Liberalism as a lunatic variety of pro-Satanic religious belief, that we can understand the way that widespread type of madness affects economy. Karl Marx, for example, became an avowed Liberal, a faithful, if perhaps unsuspecting follower of Paolo Sarpi, but, nonetheless, an avowed believer in the witchcraft cult of Adam Smith, and an unwitting, but nonetheless dutiful servant of Lord

Palmerston's Young Europe and Young America swindles.[21]

Economics & Science

Without emphasis on relevant issues of physical science, there is no competent treatment of the subject of economics.

Please do not make the terrible error of assuming that the immediately preceding remarks are to be assessed as a deprecating criticism of that Creator presented in Chapter 1 of **Genesis**. Like the Albert Einstein who praised Kepler's genius and that of Bernhard Riemann on precisely this account, I am absolutely certain of the Creator's efficient existence, as every competent

scientist is—which is to say that "I am not a Liberal." The point is, that since the Liberals absolutely do not believe in, or worship the actual Creator, nor do the so-called "fundamentalists," either, why are either of them wasting their time sitting in churches? (What awful thing, what earthly tyrant are they attempting to please?) Neither actual universal principles, nor an actual notion of a lawful process of Creation, exist for either of them. Kepler and Albert Einstein, for example, did understand. In saying these things, I am stretching nothing, nor am I wandering from the principal, stated subject matter, economics, of this report. The foundations of competent economic studies exist essentially in the physical-scientific implications of man to man in the relationship of society to the physical universe as defined, in fact, by Academician V.I. Vernadsky.

There are two leading points involved in reporting what I have referenced here as the character of Liberalism. First, those who deny Johannes Kepler's unique originality in discovering the principle of universal gravitation, are implicitly denying the existence of a Creator as being a Creator, as all followers of the myth

---

21. Britain's Engels was always an anti-American influence on Marx, as in the matter of Friedrich List, and, later, also Henry C. Carey. It was natural that Engels would appear in the 1890s as an agent of the Fabian Society, as in the case of the recruitment of Alexander Helphand (Parvus) to life-long service on behalf of the British Foreign Office. Helphand's role as a Balkans-based British arms dealer, and the orchestration of a time-sensitive, war-time trip to Finland by V.I. Lenin, did not work out fully as the British Foreign Office had intended.

Einstein on Kepler

Here are excerpts from an essay by Einstein, in commemoration of the 300th anniversary of Kepler's death. It appeared in the Frankfurter Zeitung *on Nov. 9, 1930.*

In anxious and uncertain times like ours, when it is difficult to find pleasure in humanity and the course of human affairs, it is particularly consoling to think of the serene greatness of a Kepler. Kepler lived in an age in which the reign of law in nature was by no

Ferdinand Schmutze

means an accepted certainty. How great must his faith in a uniform law have been, to have given him the strength to devote ten years of hard and patient work to the empirical investigation of the movement of the planets and the mathematical laws of that movement, entirely on his own, supported by no one and understood by very few! ...

One can never see where a planet really is at any given moment, but only in what direction it can be seen just then from the Earth, which is itself moving in an unknown manner around the Sun. The difficulties thus seemed practically unsurmountable.

Kepler had to discover a way of bringing order into this chaos.

of Isaac Newton's fraudulently claimed discovery of gravitation have done with their utterly fraudulent claim that Newton had "independently" discovered gravitation. This issue of theology, stated as I have introduced it here, is, therefore, on this account, the key to all competent insight into a science of economy.

If one listens carefully to the arguments made, on this subject of Newton's alleged discovery, by typical science-department academics over the past century, the critically significant expression in their apology for Newton, the positivists, and the existentialists, as, still today, has been "We have been taught to believe," an assertion made with the accompanying suggestion that the laying on of Laputan academic hands in blind worship of current taught opinion, proves that it is not the Creator of the universe, but silly fraud Isaac Newton, who embodies a final authority on the subject of the way in which our universe is organized.

Essentially, the discovery of the general principle of Solar gravitation was made, uniquely, by Johannes Kepler, as this discovery was presented in rigorous detail in his work whose title is properly translated into English as "The Harmonies of the World." The evidence on this point is conclusive and widely available to those who actually seek truth, rather than contemporary, prevalent, academic voodoo practices.

Kepler, a student of the work of the founder of modern scientific thought, Cardinal Nicholas of Cusa, and also of the brilliant follower of Cusa, Leonardo da Vinci, had begun his attack on the subject of the organization of the Solar system from the standpoint of the concept of *dynamics* as dynamics is presented by the ancient Pythagoreans and Plato.

At the start, Kepler had therefore adopted the view that the ordering of the bodies within the Solar system must be a rational expression of a dynamic (e.g., Pythagorean, Platonic) universe, and, therefore, must have some root-connection to the ordering principle underlying the appearance of an array of the Platonic solids. Foolish commentators propose that Kepler had later abandoned that view. Rather, being an honest and very hard-working fellow, Kepler shifted his line of investigation to other aspects of the matter, for a time, but was then compelled to return to an approximation of something functionally reflecting the Platonic solids' series. It is on the basis of that principle of harmonics that Kepler derived the exact formulation which was rudely plagiarized, without even an attempt at supporting evidence, by the circles of Isaac Newton.

At that point, the usual gossip had abandoned all serious attention to the detail of Kepler's actual discovery of the principle of gravitation, as if Albert Einstein had not traced out the empirical evidence developed by Kepler, evidence which depended upon the ironical juxtaposition of the human senses of sight and hearing. Neither sense, as a sense, could represent the experimental result of the evidence. Human sense-perceptions are merely scientific instruments, as a thermometer is a scientific instriment, which senses usually come with the package delivered with the infant at birth. Gravitation, for example, as a principle, actually exists, as Kepler demonstrated experimentally; it lies outside sense-perception as such. An instrument "counts," so to speak; what is it that is being counted?

The importance, for economy today, of this aspect of Kepler's contribution to the founding of modern science, is that Kepler came to relegate the powers of sense-perception to the status of instrumentation (e.g., harmonics), rather than an expression of the silliness of naive ontological sense-certainty. Thus, on this account, the evidence of both these senses, when correlated, reflected the physical science of the Pythagoreans and Plato, and expressed the same approach stated later in the opening two paragraphs of Bernhard Riemann's 1854 habilitation dissertation.

To appreciate that aspect of Kepler's work, it is essential to take into account the deeper implications of his concept of the infinitesimal as already determined, for Kepler's work, by the evidence of "equal areas," "equal times." This evidence had shown that the adducible infinitesimal of the orbital action was not, as the foolish Leonhard Euler was to presume later, a metrical, mathematical smallness, but an ontological matter per se, as Albert Einstein emphasized this later: something acting efficiently as if from above, and containing the motion which it expresses, always and everywhere. The principle of action is not located within the apparent evidence, but, as Einstein argued, is to be identified as the "hand" which controls the action everywhere, apparently as if "infinitesimally."

This consideration, already evident experimentally in the study of the planetary orbit itself, is to be applied to deriving a harmonic formulation for the organization of the relationship within the Solar system.[22] More significant than the fact of the harmonic determination of

---

22. Put aside the silly Laplace's (and Cauchy's) feverish passions for attempting to get three bodies into the same astronomical bed.

the function of Solar system gravitation, is the fact that the principle of action thus manifest empirically, as Kepler had shown, lies as if outside any hypothetically imaginable boundary of the system as a whole. This was stated by Einstein as defining the universe as both Keplerian and Riemannian, and as representing a universe which is self-bounded.

Since, for Einstein, the finiteness of the universe is that of an anti-entropic, expanding universe of experimental effects, we must describe the universe as either self-bounded, or *as self-bounded and also not externally bounded*. This pointed Einstein and other competent scientific thinkers, from outside the Babylonian cults of academia, to a universe as conceived as a matter of Keplerian harmonics, that in a sense of harmonics coherent with the work of Max Planck and Einstein, rather than the habits of Planck's adversaries from among the followers of Ernst Mach and later reductionist (e.g., "deconstructionist") advocates of "quantum mechanics."

These considerations, just summarized so, bring us back to a fresh view of the implications of both the influence of Paolo Sarpi, and the way in which a true science of economy, on which I rely, must situate mankind within a Keplerian universe, a universe which is to be viewed in the large from the standpoint of Kepler, Planck, and as the living universe of Russia's Academician V.I. Vernadsky. This is the framework within which any truly competent economist must situate his thinking if he, or she is to be better than very, very modestly useful in the affairs of mankind today. These considerations must be considered so before discussing the meaning of "money" under the global crisis-conditions of today.

These matters identified in this chapter will now be addressed in a relevantly more fulsome way in the course of the chapters to follow.

2. It Is Called 'Dynamics'

Now, we come to subject-matter which many readers will regard as the "most difficult part" of what I have to report on this present occasion. Despite the apparent difficulties, the matters so presented can not be avoided, if the most crucial issues of our time of crisis are to be competently understood and solved.

At its birth, what could have been called "science" in retrospect today, were better identified as *astrogation*, rather than astronomy. The evidence from an assortment of surviving ancient calendars, including one ancient one attributed to the North magnetic pole, has shown, that this knowledge of cycles of universal change could have been accumulated only through many tens of thousands of years of a fairly regular practice of a form of trans-oceanic navigation, as practiced, more or less regularly, by the maritime cultures which produced the evidence on which those calendars were based. After all that might be considered, the time required for a relevant flotilla of ships comparable to the Viking craft, or those of Ulysses' *Odyssey*, or larger, to sail from approximately the coast of present-day Portugal to the Caribbean, about six or seven thousands years ago, would have been about the same required by Christopher Columbus' first act of discovery. A habit of such odysseys, over tens of thousands of years, would have been required to develop the presently validatable, relevant evidence of the ancient mariners' experience.

This compels us to prepare our history of the development of society, by looking back deeply to the indicated onset of that last great glaciation in the northern hemisphere when, for much of that time, the oceans were about four hundred feet lower than presently, and, thus, to trace the development of civilization in the area of what had been a great frozen heap of ice, as steered by migration of ocean-going maritime cultures into the area of the land-mass emerging from under the melting ice of the glaciation, as into the Mediterranean.

No civilized geometry could have been derived from the well-known, "flat Earth" presumptions of the a-priorist Euclid, but only from a pre-Aristotelean, maritime culture governed by a practical notion of *Sphaerics* such as that adopted by the Pythagoreans. Thus, in the physical science which emerged from the work of Nicholas of Cusa, Leonardo da Vinci, and Johannes Kepler—as Bernhard Riemann, later, there are no *a-priori* presumptions allowed. Nor, as Riemann warned in that concluding sentence of his 1854 habilitation dissertation, can any *a-priori* mathematics can be treated as the foundation of a physical science.[23]

---

23. It is relevant to the function of this present report, to emphasize, that my devotion to a physical, rather than a merely mathematical geometry, was clearly established in the memories of some among my relevant classmates in both public schooling and university textbooks and classrooms from the first hour of my adolescent, introductory class in plane geometry. Challenged, routinely, by the teacher, to report to her and to the class what I thought to be important about the subject of geometry, I responded without the slightest apprehension of any cause for dispute in

The concept of dynamics, when seen in terms of both cycles in ancient astrogation, and of Leibniz's work in modern science, illustrates the absurdity of reductionist schemes such as that of Rene Descartes. On this account, the proofs of this fact already supplied by Gottfried Leibniz during the 1690s, remain conclusive for all occasions to the present moment.

The essential point thus implied by experience with the work of Gottfried Leibniz, and onward, is, that, in the actual practice of physical science, with certain crucially important qualifications, the future has always pre-determined the present, that in a certain way; but, also, that the human will, when acting, presently, under certain conditions and in a certain way, can predetermine the selection of that principle which would change the efficient expression of a future from what it would have been otherwise. Such, exactly, is implicit in the strict definition of any experimentally validatable universal physical principle, such as Kepler's uniquely original scientific discovery of universal gravitation.

One of the simplest expressions of this functional notion of the future is the role of those aspects of basic economic infrastructure which pre-shape the effective expression of productive effort as relative productivity, as distinct from current direct action on the production-process. Another expression, is the effect of employing a newly discovered universal physical principle. Another expression is those changes in practiced education policy which represent an increase of the potential for discoveries of principle within a population so educated.

This definition does not mean that everything in the universe is simply predetermined in that way; rather, it means that mankind may be able to change the effect on the present, of the future state of the universe, as by aid of discovery of universal principles, in the here and now: thus effecting a seemingly miraculous change from that future state which would have been pre-determined, had man not, previously, willfully intervened, once more, in a certain new way, as by introduction of a newly discovered universal physical principle to human practice. This, however, is subject to the condition that individual persons discover the principles which permit this kind of change *in the future* to occur as a voluntary change in principle in the present.

Compare this view with *Genesis* 1. The Creator and mankind share existence in the present's ultimate future. This existence must be realized as a willfully efficient connection. We are the presently acting image of an efficient form of ultimately immortal existence in that future which is termed "the simultaneity of eternity." So, we should be judged, we are. On this point, we must not permit blind faith in mere sense-certainty to cause us to deceive ourselves.

The Malthusian Cults

The relevant, great problem for most of mankind, thus far in known history, is that, as the point is illustrated by dramatist Aeschylus' *Prometheus Bound*, most cultures presently known to us from what are termed ancient, medieval, and modern histories, have had many characteristics of oligarchical systems, in which scientific and related progress is intentionally suppressed, as *Prometheus Bound* illustrates the case. Most of these cultures, such as the empires of Southwest Asia, and the Roman and Norman empires, and modern religious cults, have employed prohibitions, such as that of the drama's Olympian Zeus, and created mystery cults and religions, to prevent humanity from gaining access to usable knowledge of universal physical principles.

These prohibitions and related practices to the same intended effect, as in schools and universities in the U.S.A. and Europe today, are intended to suppress those kinds of scientific and related knowledge which would tend to promote what the ruling oligarchies consider undesirable increases of populations, or to lead to cessation of the reign of oligarchies over subject popu-

---

my statement: "To make supporting structures stronger" through what could be seen as apparent holes in the supporting structures. What I reported thus, was the fruit of visits to the nearby Charlestown Navy Yard, where construction in progress had clearly conveyed that conclusion to me. My subsequent, decades-long quarrel with taught secondary and university mathematics, first discovered its proper nesting-place in early 1953, in my solid commitment to the outlook and method of Bernhard Riemann's 1854 habilitation dissertation. The true origin of my adolescent views on mathematics was the coincidence of a Navy Yard visit's experience with significant sampling from English translations of the work of Gottfried Leibniz, in my opposition to Descartes at that time. From that point in time on, my standpoint in this and related matters was never formal, but, rather, ontological. During my adolescence and later, I was repeatedly astonished that so many among my classmates could have accepted the classroom sophistries of *"self-evident"* mathematics as science. Hence, my related social discomforts in those schools, were balanced against the greater intellectual rewards of possessing the authority of original discovery of a repeatedly demonstrable proof of principle. For me, the essence of science is standing up for truth, whether the truth were liked by my putative peers, or not.

lations. The bans on knowledge are not imposed because such knowledge would not be understandable by the population, but, on the contrary, because, the ruling oligarchs fear that it were much too easily mastered by the population unless the population were prevented from making the discoveries of which it were capable, but for "mass-brainwashing," or other measures to the same general effect by our contemporary, pro-genocide. dupes of the malthusians Prince Philip of the pro-genocidal World Wildlife Fund, and Philip's dupe and former U.S. Senator Al Gore.

The actual motive for Malthusian and related sorts of cultish practices of induced stupidity among masses of people, such as the cult of "global warming" today, has always been, in known history of mankind, the fear among a ruling oligarchy, that increase of efficient knowledge of universal physical, or related kinds of principles, among the general population, would be a threat to the continued power to rule by the oligarchy. Since technological and social progress of the population is driven by the need of a growing population to increase its level of potential population-density, the increase of such knowledge among the population has always been the cause of great fear, and related rage, among such specimens of the usual oligarchical class as the Duke of Edinburgh, the leader of the World Wildlife Fund, who intends to stupefy the world's population to such a degree that the present world population of about six and a half billions persons, could be rapidly reduced to about two, or even less. Thus, both, speaking frankly, Hitler-like "population reduction" and "zero- technological-growth" cults, such as those of "environmentalism" and "globalization" of Prince Philip and others today, which have become endemically characteristic features of the known oligarchical models of society.

That, for example, is the underlying, oligarchical motive for the lying assertion of Isaac Newton's discovery of gravitation which has been circulated by the virtual Babylonian priesthood governing the leading universities and other institutions still today. It is the model for what the Nazi regime did to Jews within its reach, and also intended to accomplish against other populations, such as Slavs in general.

EIRNS/James Rea

"The actual motive for Malthusian and related sorts of cultish practices of induced stupidity among masses of people," LaRouche writes, "such as the cult of 'global warming' today, has always been, in known history of mankind, the fear among a ruling oligarchy, that increase of efficient knowledge of universal physical, or related kinds of principles, among the general population, would be a threat to the continued power to rule by the oligarchy." Here, a rally in Washington in 2007.

The oligarchical model, thus, defends itself with what are essentially the twin forces of awful fear and superstitions. That model represents a corruption of mind and morality which often takes the form of Dionysian terrorism, as in the case of the frankly fascist, Dionysiac outbursts of the so-called "Sixty-Eighters." The principal target of those oligarchical chains of fears and superstitions, is the crippling of the cognitive powers of the individual human mind among most members of the populations as a whole. .

Thus, as I shall stress, it is with awareness of that implication of oligarchical models, that, in this chapter, my subject is the underlying implication of *dynamic potential* for the population's increasing knowledge of universal principles of practice. At this point in this report, some useful, if preliminary insight, can be provided to the reader, along the following lines.

Economic Forecasting as Such

What I have just identified in these preceding paragraphs, is that this is the principle of *dynamics* which underlines competent approaches to economic forecasting of potential future states of the universe. It has been for precisely this reason, that I have been, repeatedly, a successful long-range economic forecaster where all of my putative rivals have failed, repeatedly. I repeat, therefore: it is the notion of that quality of action on the future, to change it, through which we must foresee a *predetermination* of a future change, rather than the presumption of those incompetent economic forecasters (for example) who indulge in what passes for what is, in practice, the virtually inevitably failed, past-oriented statistical practice, of so-called "statistical forecasting:" I mean forecasting on the basis of considering only the experience of the present acquired up to some present time. It is precisely in this ability of the human mind on which I have come to rely, that we must locate the existence of that quality of creativity's potential which distinguishes the individual member of the human species categorically from all lower forms of life.

We must foresee the consequences of attrition similarly. Not only does technological attrition have the effect of "wear and tear." Failure to advance the level of technology, or failure to increase the capital-intensity of production and infrastructure per capita and per square kilometer, mean attrition, as such negligence turns back the "clock of the future" on mankind.

It is notable, that these aforesaid considerations have been the primary considerations in my method of economic forecasting. Capital-investment cycles, including consideration of the rates of scientific- technological investment in increased physical capital-intensity, per capita and per square-kilometer, have been paramount considerations in the qualitative superiority of my forecasts, when those of all putative rivals have been more or less disastrously wrong.

Albert Einstein would, most probably, agree, and according to a fair reading of the best available evidence, most probably did.[24]

What I have just written in these preceding paragraphs, can, and, probably should be restated in the following way.

'A Simultaneity of Eternity'

Nothing I have written here thus far can be read as a denial of an ontologically real, efficient existence of the future's control over the present. In adopting discovered universal physical principles, or the like, we are redefining the future consequences of our present actions. This is to speak of discovered universal physical principles, or the principle summed up in the concluding paragraph of Percy B. Shelley's ***In Defence of Poetry***. In one such type of case, we have introduced the practice of a newly adopted universal physical principle, such as Kepler's uniquely original discovery of the principle of Solar gravitation. In another type of case, we have introduced a change of principle in the way in which a culture thinks about the way it chooses to govern its behavior.

What the reader must take into account, however, is that our definition of an actual future here, is remarkably different than the ignorant, so-called "common sense" reading of that specific choice of language would ordinarily recommend. What I am pointing out is, in fact, not unknown to relevant Christian theologians, for example; it is a conception to which I have frequently referred in my own earlier writings, but also emphasized by relevant other persons. It is the concept of what is named as "the simultaneity of eternity," as such a Platonic principle is illustrated by Raphael Sanzio's "The School of Athens."

The concept may be identified by the following descriptions. This is another mode for stating the notion of the principle of dynamics, as this ancient principle of the Pythagoreans and Plato was revived by Gottfried Leibniz during the 1690s. It is the same principle, as developed further by Bernhard Riemann, which has been the foundation of my relatively extraordinary success as a long-range forecaster in my work of the 1956-2008 interval to date, as my forecasting came more into public view since 1956, especially since August 1971.

The existence of the real future of mankind's universe lies along a physical-dimensional "line" called (human) *creativity*, a notion which might be identified

---

24. The internal history of modern physical science underwent a ruinous crisis from the closing decades of the Nineteenth Century to the present. That period of worsening crisis, and flagrant frauds, in the practice of and university teaching of modern physical science as such is centered around the controversy between Albert Einstein and Max Planck, on the one side, and the adepts in the positivist cults of Ernst

Mach and the followers of Bertrand Russell on the other.

Details from "The School of Athens," by Raphael Sanzio, 1510. On the left, Socrates and Aristotle are counterposed; on the right is the "Archimedes group" (Archimedes is the one using a compass to demonstrate a concept in geometry). The complete mural shows a vibrant dialogue of scientists and artists across the ages—"in the simultaneity of eternity."

by the technical term *anti-entropy*.[25] In this view, the existence of the universal future exists not at a fixed point in future time, but, rather, as if it were a wave of change in place and choice of ultimate destination, a change over which mankind can exert willful control by the future, on the present. Mankind's inventions to this effect, promote the effect of changing the existing universe, by changing the ultimate destination of mankind's existence. Think of this as an existential wave passing through an expanding universe, a universe whose future is expanding qualitatively, rather than merely quantitatively.

This can be seen as expressed in terms of new, higher states of existence in the universe, or phase-space of reference. Such qualitative developments are most typical of the conception of anti-entropy.

Restate what I have written, up to this point, here, as follows. Now, however, where the prior definition of "future" had defined mankind's available destiny as

relatively fixed, as statistical forecasters do, a correct view, now, is that a new, qualitatively changed "future" is, or will be acting, *as if from the future*, upon the present—for the better, or worse. The principle of dynamics as employed by Leibniz, Riemann, and Einstein holds sway; but we must add the qualification, the "added dimensionality," that the future itself, as future is typified for physical science by Kepler's uniquely original discovery of the principle of universal gravitation, is changing qualitatively, such that the future acting upon us today, is a different future-point than that of the day before. However, we, in turn, are acting upon what had been the earlier future-point, to generate the new, "more distant" future-point in physical space-time, that defined in what may be usefully termed "anti-entropic" (i.e., "actual") physical space-time.

To repeat the point for the sake of clarity: the future does act on the present, and the present does act to change that future which is acting on the present. If that appears to confuse some readers, it is, chiefly, because those readers' minds are still stuck in the proverbial mud of sense-certainty.

Do we actually know this to be the case in practice? As one typical professor said: "Can we actually know

---

25. "Negative entropy" is a misleading term; the appropriate term is "anti-entropy." The idea of a mathematical-physics controversy, over entropy versus negative entropy, introduced by the followers of Clausius and Grassmann, was always, essentially, a neo-Cartesian hoax, a failure to grasp the implications of Leibniz's systematic exposure of the frauds of Rene Descartes.

it—can we prove it, rather than merely believe it,"[26] as some arbitrary presumption of some odd religious belief, such as those of the true believers in Descartes, Ernst Mach, or the followers of Bertrand Russell? The answer should be, "Yes. We already know it, and could prove it; because the creative powers of the human mind, as distinct from the characteristics of all lower forms of life, practice that effect upon the universe, and, thus, upon the dynamical future-point which locates (generates) the modified universe in which we must exist and act today."

To restate this crucial fact: when mankind adopts a discovered principle of the universe within the embrace of society's practical intentions, the universe is changed in its expressed intention. The future so newly defined, not only as we perceive it, but as our changed choices of methods of actions, now acts to define those effects which the present experiences as the reaction to the present by the future.

A Relevant Case

The death of President Franklin Roosevelt, inasmuch as that brought the reversal of his policies, and of the directions of policy-shaping under President Truman, caused a sudden and worsening decline in the future prospects of the United States, and, also, civilization world-wide. The changes in direction of policy made possible through the assassination of President John F. Kennedy, unleashed a downward direction in long-ranging policy-shaping which led into the phenomenon of the gross cultural-moral decadence of international "68ers," with such immediate consequences as the coming of the Nixon Administration, and the consequent long wave of decline in the economy and culture of the U.S.A., the Americas generally, and Europe, which has continued to the present day.

Mankind as such is an integral, willful factor of governing principles in the universe around us. The principle which distinguishes mankind from lower forms of life is an integral part of the physical universe we inhabit. Our choices of principled direction of decision-making, and of institutions, are an integral, willful part of the physical universe which we inhabit.

"How, actually, could we know this character of our future—in economy, or otherwise?" An appropriate answer to that question would be: "We know this if we act on our domain in that way." This is the method which I have employed since I first really began to understand the implications of Bernhard Riemann's work for a practiced science of physical economy, in early 1953. This is the basis on which I forecast the proverbial, hypergeometric "wave of the future;" and, if you read my crucial economic forecasts as I have cast them (not as "predictions" of a Cartesian type), so far, I have never been mistaken in what I actually claimed, and that with an exceptionally careful representation. Once I had also grasped the implications of Academician V.I. Vernadsky's leading discoveries in physical biochemistry a few decades ago, my advantage was greatly amplified by insight into the principled implications of the categorical evidence on which the notions of Biosphere and Noösphere depend.

The choices of direction of policy-shaping, such as changes in popular culture, are the generation of changes in the principled character of the physical universe which we inhabit. These choices change, thus, the way in which our inhabited physical domain acts and reacts upon us.

That much said thus far, I shall now restate the same point somewhat differently, for the reader's sake.

From the Standpoint of Technology

Compare the case as I have just summarily described it, with a view of the same matters from the vantage-point of the historical-line of technological rise in the frontier of technology represented by increases in mankind's willful command of, and use of increases in what is termed "energy-flux density." That the same number of calories expressed in a leap to a certain higher level of energy-flux density, performs a higher quality of work (effect on the universe) than the number of counted calories at a lower energy-flux density.[27]

So. the rise in energy-density-cross-section per square centimeter, has an effect which is an echo of a "future line" of the sort to which I have referred above.

---

26. Cf. *The Harvard Yard*, https://archive.org/details/LaRouchePAC-TheHarvardYard191

27. It is now approximately 318 years since Gottfried Leibniz proved the fraudulent character of the methods and conclusions of Rene Descartes. Yet, some leading members of the U.S. Congress and many persons misnamed as accredited scientists are still basing their cultish "environmentalist" frauds, as on the definition of "energy," on the fraud of Descartes, still today. Some of these fools are called "scientists."

To the degree that society takes advantage of such a gain, the productive powers of labor per capita and per square kilometer, are increased qualitatively. This works to such effect that if we compare the human species' potential relative population-density with that of the higher apes, man's power to raise the intensity of the realized energy-flux-density of human action (qualitatively) per capita and per square kilometer, shows the human species to be free of the principled limits to population-growth of all inferior species.

Vernadsky has been most valuable in emphasizing a comparable phenomenon in the relative increase of living processes over intrinsically non-living ones, and of the human species' Noösphere above the phase-spatial systems of all other living species combined.

When we view these matters as expressing a general principle within our universe, we have the scent of the higher principle which I am discussing here. In other words: there is a principle more or less comparable to the notion of *qualitative anti-entropy* (e.g., new dimensions in physical space-time created), a principle which is also expressed by the potential of the mind of the individual member of the human species, to "expand the universe" qualitatively. This expansion defines the "current wave of the future" which is acting reciprocally, and dynamically upon our present. We, in turn, by aid of those of our potential noëtic powers which are absent in all lower forms of individual life, are able, potentially, to shift that "wave of the future" upward. This works to the effect that all of our actions, even those which appear to be unchanged forms of individual practice, are changed in character *dynamically*, reflecting the change in the character of the universe's future which has been effected by some relevant action upon society generally, by some creative action performed by the individual human will, by means of (speaking theologically) the divine soul, in the likeness of that of the Creator, of the human individual, a soul absent in all other known living creatures.

Mind or Sense-Perception?

The troubling aspect of the case which I have just outlined above, should be recognized as an effect of a Euclidean-like acceptance of belief in mythical notions of the existence of an a-priorism attributed to human sense-certainty. Once we accept the experimentally demonstrated actuality, as Kepler did for the effects of universal gravitation, that sense-perceptions are never better than shadows which have been cast by a real universe upon an imagined universe, we are rightly impelled to force our mind—the real, cognitive mind—to block out the habit of blind faith in sensations, and to ask ourselves what kind of an object might have cast those shadows, as Kepler did in discovering the actual principle of gravitation in harmonic orderings. Thus, for example, the succession of the rejection of the principle of harmonics governing the determination of gravitation, was greatly aggravated by the degeneration of modern science brought about through the influence of the respective mechanistic and rabid dogmas of Ernst Mach and Bertrand Russell in degrading the discovery of the harmonic principle by Max Planck.

Essentially, this means, ontologically, defining the real universe as the one which casts those shadows which we can qualify, experimentally, as principles of the same class of types as Kepler's discovery of gravitation.

Now, when that correction of the systemic errors of what is still, presently popular, even most academic opinion, has been made, the human mind is enabled to see matters of scientific principle more or less as Bernhard Riemann, Albert Einstein and Max Planck did, or as Cardinal Nicholas of Cusa did in such seminal writings on modern science as his **De Docta Ignorantia**, or as the follower of Cusa, Johannes Kepler, did in Kepler's uniquely original discovery, in his **The Harmonies of the World**, of a universal principle of gravitation.

From that higher vantage-point of viewing our universe, the notion of the true universal actuality is typified by the principle which Albert Einstein adduced from his review-in-depth of Kepler's discovery of the universal principle of gravitation. Review that matter as follows.

As I have repeatedly emphasized in earlier locations, the first key to Kepler's uniquely original discovery in the matter of the principle of gravitation, was the measurement of "equal areas, equal times." In the effort to express each single cycle as motion in an arbitrarily small portion of that cycle, there was no satisfactory kind of existing measurement. It was necessary to define the physical function mathematically by what subsumed the cycle, rather than as by a function of action in the small. However, when Kepler attempted to define the subsuming function for a set of physical planetary orbits similarly defined, it was necessary to define a principle which subsumed the organization of the set of orbits of which the Solar System as a whole might be defined. This led Kepler to recognize that no ordinary algebraic solution existed; rather, it was necessary to define the relevant harmonic function underlying the relationship among the orbital pathways. The required solution was one lying outside the domain of the sensory images of either sight or sound. No sense-organ other than the creative powers of the human mind itself, would suffice.

Einstein's response to Kepler's presentation was that Kepler's formulation for the Solar System's expression of universal gravitation presented the case of a self-contained universe, which was, therefore, finite, but without an external boundary. While this does not exclude the existence of other universal physical principles, which also define a universe similarly, it defines the proper meaning of the use of the term universal principles, as principles which are to be similarly defined as lying outside the domain of mathematics as such. Therefore, Kepler's proof, as presented by him in his *The Harmonies of the World*, defined the proper meaning of all uses of the term universal physical principle as principles lying outside the domain of mathematics as such. Thus, Einstein emphasized that Kepler's universe was already Riemannian in quality, and that all competent physical science must be premised on that same quality of conception.

3. Physical-Economic, Or Other Values? What Is Your Future?

The foregoing considerations must guide the adoption of any principled notion of economic policy by, and among nations presently. After all, we inhabit a universe so defined as to require this approach. We must now translate what has been said here, above, into the language and practice of a science of physical economy. The considerations which have been treated here until now, provide the "platform" from which we are enabled to make a competent entry into that branch of physical science properly named a science of physical economy.

Within the preceding chapters we have considered the elements of physical science as broadly stated in a relatively elementary way. With the successive discoveries of principle by, most notably, such followers of Nicholas of Cusa as Johannes Kepler, Fermat, and Leibniz, modern European civilization gained those notions which formed the uniquely modern scientific method of the Leibniz calculus. These accomplishments, by Leibniz, of the most immediate relevance for our argument here, were, successively: the concept of the calculus as such, circa 1676; at the close of the Seventeenth Century and the beginning of the Eighteenth, the establishing of a competently anti-Cartesian conception of physical science; and, the consequent notions of a principle of physical least action.

All of these stages of Leibniz's discoveries were derived from the general conception of the so-called "infinitesimal." This was the notion, derived from the combined effects of the discoveries of Kepler and Fermat, of universal physical principles as "enclosing" the universe of our experience, rather than being mere measurements within the framework of an a-priori preconception of a universe. This conception of the "infinitesimal calculus," by Leibniz, depended crucially upon Kepler's discovery of a principle of universal gravitation, rather than a-priori notions such as Euclid's, as enclosing action observed within the universe. This is the conception of an anti-Euclidean geometry, as drawn out more fully in Bernhard Riemann's 1854 habilitation dissertation.[28]

These were the foundations of notions of a science of physical economy which informed the founding of the modern, Leibnizian economic science of physical economy, as developed through the work of the Ecole Polytechnique of Gaspard Monge and Lazare Carnot. The next leap forward in this domain was accomplished, chiefly, by Bernhard Riemann, beginning his 1854 habilitation dissertation; this was the first leap into that "purely physical" anti-Euclidean geometry which had been already anticipated in Kepler's uniquely original discovery of the principle of universal gravitation.

The importance of this point is so crucial for all competent science, including economic science, that we must emphasize the relevant connections once more, here.

As emphasized above, the definition of meaning of

---

28. Not non-Euclidean!

"universal physical principle," or, said simply, a "universal principle" of any quality, must be a principle which encloses, rather than merely "connects points within" the universe, or the phase-space of the universe under consideration. It may also connect points within the universe, but that connection may occur only as a subsumed expression of its essential character as enclosing the universe, or relevant qualitative phase-space.

Basic Economic Infrastructure

Typical of this is the notion of the function of basic economic infrastructure. That is a notion which does not exist in the crippled mental processes of today's

---

Fermat's Principle

The following is excerpted from EIR, *Dec. 23, 2005. The* full text *is available.*

What the reason was for the change in light's direction when passing from one medium to another was a major fight in the 17th Century, and it must become so, again, today. Pierre de Fermat's principle that light's action is determined by the principle of quickest time, was a political statement, a clear attack on the prevalent empiricist thinking, and a call back to the method of Greek knowledge. It demanded a conception of physical science that places man in his proper place—as in the image of, and participating in a single Creation, overthrowing the oligarchical view that placed man infinitely below the incomprehensible caprice of the Olympian gods and human feudal lords.

The refractive behavior of light had been a source of study and consternation for centuries, since no simple relationship between the angles of incidence and refraction could be determined (see diagram). It was in 1621, that the Dutch investigator Willebrord Snell determined that it is the sines of the angles of incidence and refraction that maintain a constant ratio for a given pair of media, an experiment that is worth carrying out yourself.

Although Snell is correct, this observation of effects does not address itself to cause. Descartes, insisting that light had to be understood as ballistic particles (in opposition to Leonardo da Vinci, and to keep his own purely mechanical outlook) was forced to conclude, erroneously, that light actually sped up upon entering water. He also claimed Snell's discovery as his own! Fermat found this speeding up to be absurd, and sought to determine the *cause* for light's behavior.

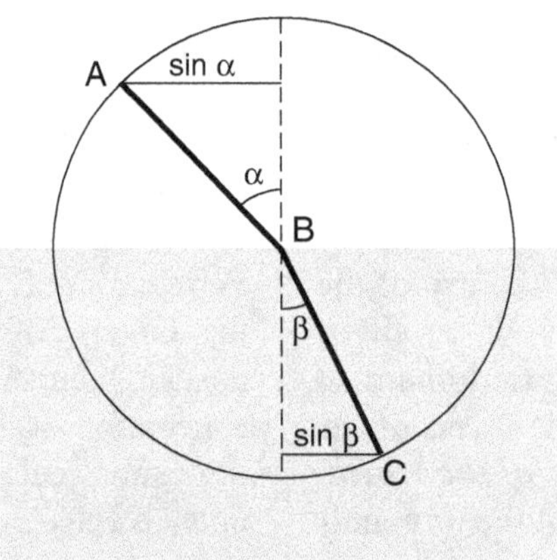

Snell determined that the ratio sin/α : sin/β is maintained for two media, no matter at what angle the light hits the boundary.

To note the sine relationship is good, but to actually assert that this trend *is* a scientific principle would not be an honest blunder, it would be an admission by anyone who would make that statement, that that person believes principles are unknowable.[1]

Fermat sought not to describe the motion of the fish, but the shape of the aquarium in which they swam: He returned to the Greek discovery that light reflected off a mirror takes the path of minimal distance, an experiment worth performing on your own.

Fermat took up this approach, and hypothesized and demonstrated in 1662 that light follows a path of quickest *time*, rather than shortest distance: As far as the light is concerned, it is always propagating straight ahead by this principle. This hypothesis results in the sine ratio discovered by Snell, but Fermat *delivered* the child whose form Snell accurately reported....

—Jason Ross

---

1. One could just as well make the (admittedly, true) statement that middle schoolers with larger feet are better spellers. Larger feet do not confer orthographic proficiency; the education that comes with being older does. Retrospective musings on the results of completed action in the past are not hypotheses of motive powers.

customary opinion, whether in today's law-making practices, or in generally accepted, but scientifically incompetent, accounting practice. In any competent form of practice of national income accounting, basic economic infrastructure is that which efficiently encloses, functionally, the real action in which particular productive action or a productive effect is generated. This "enclosing" performs the function of amplifying, or diminution, of the action which it "encloses."

Wasteful practices (and expenditures) which do not meet that standard (such as imposition of tolls, as a substitute for public funding, as distinct from taxation to support public infrastructure) are not competently classed as being required infrastructure, since, expressed in that form, they make no assured net, effective contribution to a productive action. So, on this account, tax-revenue derived from legalized gambling, is a destructive form of utter waste.

Similarly, the substitution of solar panels and windmills for nuclear-fission powered sources is inherently a net waste, with no actual net benefit to any economy. It is the relative energy-flux density of sources and application of power which determines the relative value of power produced for society. "Soft energy" is for "Luddites" and similarly "soft-headed" fools. These "soft-headed" modes are not merely foolish; they are viciously destructive, and also actually pro-genocidal in their effects on the conditions of human life.

Riemannn & Vernadsky in Economy

It was indispensable for the founding of a modern science of physical economy, that, as Riemann prescribed in his habilitation dissertation, we must free science from the grip of any formal mathematics which depended upon a-priori assumptions. It is properly required that we derive mathematics from physical principles, rather than attributing the authority of physical principles to any a-priori assumptions, such as those of mere mathematics, respecting human individual sense-perceptions. We must think of mathematical representations in purely physical-experimental terms, rather than the other way around. This objective for mathematics, as physical mathematics, was realized in essentials by the discoveries of Bernhard Riemann.

Any mathematical system for physics which evades that challenge presented by Riemann, is intrinsically incompetent, especially so for any attempt to adduce the physical principles governing growth or failure in modern economy. Competence does not permit the way in which ivory-tower fantasists seek a mathematical-statistical rule for economy; competence requires primary attention to the role of implementation of discoveries of universal principles in determining the anti-entropic increase, or entropic collapse of physical economies so defined.

There are, however, certain additional considerations which governments must emphasize now, if a very early, general breakdown of the present economy of the entire planet is to be averted. Most significant is, as I have emphasized this principle in earlier locations, Academician V.I. Vernadsky's notion of three distinct, subsumed categories of universal physical principle: the *abiotic*, the *Biosphere*, and the *Noösphere*. These are the respectively unique categories which presently compose our conscious experience of the existence of the universe as a whole; but, these are also each an essential component of the whole subject-matter of a science of physical economy. No presently competent representation of the subject of physical economy could exist if it did not consider all three distinct categories of functional existence in cohering functional terms of reference.

Therefore, the most important consideration to be emphasized is that living processes can not be derived from non-living, and cognitive processes can not be derived from any known living processes other than the human individual.[29] Most notably, for precisely this reason, any effort to constrain the practice of economy within reductionist assumptions inherent in the empiricist methods of such as Adam Smith and Smith's follower Karl Marx, must lead toward general disaster, and do, unless they are aborted in time to prevent that lurking outcome. Marx's method is just as good, and even significantly better than that of Marx's teacher Adam Smith; but, both share in common certain erroneous axiomatic-like presumptions, as identified by Marx as his adopted views, which must, in fact, ultimately mislead the believer

---

29. There is no reported, direct connection between the quality of human reason and those aspects of the human brain-process which are traced to the biology of lower forms of life. For the moment, here, it were safe to proceed as if this distinctly human cognitive power were something into which the human biological apparatus is as if "tuned," but lower forms of life not.

into disaster, as this fact is being experienced on a grandly calamitous scale of mass-insanity, as being experienced throughout most of our planet presently. As in the Soviet case, Marx's influence, like that of the Adam Smith on whom he leaned so much, effectively denied even the bare existence of the function of creativity at the point of production, just as President Richard Nixon's administration joined with its similarly deranged 68ers, in destroying the factor of physical creativity in even maintaining a previously established level of performance in the U.S. economy.

The fact of the hereditary equivalence of the monstrously destructive effect of "green" ideology on the physical economy of Earth, and the correlation of that pathological outlook with the anti-nuclear lunacy, goes to the heart of the way in which the U.S.A. and Europe have destroyed themselves physically-economically during the past forty years. Any continuation of the influence of that "green," anti-nuclear ideology now would send civilization tumbling into the life-expectancies and behavioral characteristics of the baboons (probably, even the baboons would shun us).

Vernadsky's discoveries, when combined with Albert Einstein's and Max Planck's conceptions of the way in which Kepler and Riemann set the conceptual foundations of all competent directions in modern science, are, presently, the unique key to defining a competent direction in organization of a general recovery of the presently disintegrating economy of the planet in its entirety today.

However, another crucial consideration must be added among those which must be taken into account in functional terms. I explain this as follows.

NASA

"To what degree," LaRouche asks, "does the continued successful direction in existence of the Solar system depend upon a function intended to be performed by present and future mankind?" Here, astronaut Rick Mastracchio conducts an Extra Vehicular Activity, an operation on the side of the International Space Station, 2007.

The Role of Man In The Solar System

Science does not simply exist. Knowledge and practice of scientific progress, and of the continued existence of mankind, depend upon the distinctly special nature of the human being, as distinct from any different form of life. It is here, on this view of human nature, that the existence of a science of economy, that any competent accounting for the existence of human economic function depends.

At first glance, the progress of mankind's conditions of life depends upon the Biosphere, which also depends upon the abiotic domain of planet Earth. This dependency includes some extremely ironical aspects. This fact should not astonish us, once we have recognized that everything respecting mankind's existence and role in the universe, insofar as we know it, is most extremely ironical.[30]

The corollary is located in the following question: to what degree does the continued successful direction in existence of the Solar system depend upon a function intended to be performed by present and future mankind?

For example, the primary source of our day to day power to exist on this planet is the Sun. Not only is the Sun the largest part of the Solar System, but virtually all known parts of the System are products of the Sun's self-development, including the radiation on which life on Earth depends. Yet, on this very account, the Sun tends to be a disappointment for us, since solar radiation would be as much a pestilence as an asset, unless we converted Solar power into products of chlorophyll without ever pausing at a solar collector or quixotic windmill.

---

30. As I have referenced this in a note above.

New Opera Production in the Verdi Tuning with a Furtwängler Touch

by Benjamin Lylloff

Sept. 3—In July and August of 2018, the Swedish opera company "Operafabriken," led by Swedish soprano Leena Malkki-Guignard, set out to create a unique stage performance of Vincenzo Bellini's 1831 opera *Norma*, performed in the scientific pitch of A=432 Hz, known as the Verdi tuning. It was performed twice at the Ystad Theater in Sweden, twice at the Helsinore Theatre House in Denmark, and once at the Malmö Palladium in Sweden. The production was the first stage performance of *Norma* in the Verdi tuning outside of Italy since the Second World War.

Performance at 432 Hz of finale "Qual cor" of Norma, *Act 2, by Vincenzo Bellini, in Helsingör, with Jochen Heibertshausen conducting.*

Malkki-Guignard brought in German conductor Jochen Heibertshausen and Italian violinist Gian Marco Sanna, to allow these artists to add their special insights and talents to the project. All three had come to know each other through the Schiller Institute Verdi-tuning campaign and had recently performed together at the Schiller Institute conference in Bad Soden, Germany. Heibertshausen has worked to grasp the general musical understanding of Wilhelm Furtwängler and has applied Furtwängler's conducting method in practice. Sanna leads the Geminiani string ensemble, in London, which plays exclusively in the Verdi tuning of A=432 Hz. The production, though on a small budget, was fully staged, complete with scenery, costumes, and lighting. It was performed with a chamber orchestra of thirteen musicians. A video of the overture is available. Malkki-Guignard sang the title role, Norma. The rest of the cast consisted of singers from Sweden and Denmark, and one singer from Georgia.

The whole project was designed to be a great learning experience. It provided a significant challenge to all the musicians and was for some, perhaps, a cultural shock. The Verdi tuning gave the singers the freedom to perform without forcing their voices and gave the orchestra a rounder and less piercing sound. Scientific research indicates that the tuning of the instruments to C=256, or approximately A=432, aligns the voice with the natural harmonics of the human singing voice.

Heibertshausen added yet another dimension. He wanted people to understand the Furtwänglerian approach. Furtwängler never conducted in the "point" but rather he conducted the preparation of the note. With that mode of conducting, the musicians do not react to impulses but are rather breathing and acting in the same moment as the conductor. That gives the conductor the ability to shape the music spontaneously; however, it requires the utmost attention from all players. Nothing essentially is mechanical. Furtwängler's demand as to the orchestral sound—as introduced in the opera performance by Heibertshausen—proved to be a great challenge. With this attention to the preparation, comes also care that each note be played in a singing way, all the way through. Singing—meaning *bel canto* with vibrato and depth, even in soft passages. It took the musicians a long time to unlearn some of their own performing habits, but when they all came together with this method, the small chamber orchestra sounded much bigger. There were moments in the music that one can only describe as something that could not have been rehearsed.

The confusion and challenge posed by this method came not just within the production but also afterwards in response to a video that was posted on Facebook of a clip from of the performances. A viewer complained in a comment that the sound of the orchestra came before Heibertshausen's downbeat, saying that he was treating the orchestra as if it were a mirror. A fair answer, I believe, is given by Dr. Hans Keller who, in a short film about Furtwängler, comments on critics' view of Furtwängler as being imprecise: "The criticism is justified but the evaluation isn't." Indeed, this apparent mirroring is the shaping of the music by the conductor and the orchestra in the same moment, which looks at times as if the orchestra is ahead of the conductor—something that would appear to be impossible in music making. But it is rather like a performance of a string quartet, in which all four players are completely together and yet, still can create in the spur of the moment.

For the opera singers and the musicians, it took four performances before this approach had firmly settled in with the performers. It was then, at that fourth performance, that pure magic moments arose, which made one think of those sonorous and organic recordings of Furtwängler.

This opera project was a good start for what one can describe as a more truthful and scientific striving towards beauty in Classical art, and there will hopefully be much more to come from these bold musicians.